THE BUTCHER

Ireland Into Film

Series editors:
Keith Hopper (text) and Gráinne Humphreys (images)

Ireland Into Film is the first project in a number of planned collaborations between Cork University Press and the Irish Film Institute. The general aim of this publishing initiative is to increase the critical understanding of 'Irish' Film (i.e. films made in, or about, Ireland). This particular series brings together writers and scholars from the fields of Film and Literary Studies to examine notable adaptations of Irish literary texts.

Other titles available in this series:

Ireland Into Film

THE BUTCHER BOY

Colin MacCabe

in association with
THE IRISH FILM INSTITUTE

First published in 2007 by
Cork University Press
Cork
Ireland

British Library Cataloguing in Publication Data
A CIP catalogue record for this book is available from the British Library.

ISBN 978-185918-286-4

Typesetting by Red Barn Publishing, Skeagh, Skibbereen

Printed by ColourBooks Ltd, Baldoyle, Dublin

Ireland Into Film receives financial assistance from
the Arts Council/An Chomhairle Ealaíon and the Irish Film Institute

For my mother, Ruth MacCabe
(née MacAdorey) a.k.a. Ward

Galleys of the Lochlanns ran here to beach, in quest of prey, their bloodbeaked prows riding low on a molten pewter surf. Danevikings, torcs of tomahawks aglitter on their breasts when Malachi wore the collar of gold. A school of turlehide whales stranded in hot noon, spouting, hobbling in the shallows. Then from the starving cagework city a horde of jerkined dwarfs, my people, with flayers' knives, running, scaling, hacking in green blubbery whalemeat. Famine, plagues and slaughters. Their blood is in me, their lust my waves. (James Joyce, *Ulysses*, 1922)

CONTENTS

LIST OF ILLUSTRATIONS

Acknowledgements

My first debt is to Patrick McCabe and Neil Jordan who were generous with both their time and their papers. In particular I must mention the unpublished novel 'Baby Pig' and the five drafts of the screenplay. All unsourced quotations from Jordan and McCabe are taken from conversations in the period November 2004 to February 2006. I hope this essay provides a useful coda to both novel and film. Diarmuid McKeown was a great ally.

I am also grateful to John Boorman, Ian Christie, Steve Woolley, Stephen Rea and Sinead O'Connor, who all talked to me as I was finishing this book. Any quotations from them are from those conversations.

Almost all my preparatory work was for class – three under-graduate courses on the films of Neil Jordan that I taught for Pitt in London in the autumn terms 2002–2004 and a graduate course on adaptation which I taught in Pittsburgh in spring 2005. I owe much to the students, who made these courses both enjoyable and stimulating.

I must also acknowledge a debt to two of my graduate students Gillian Kerr and Dana Och, particularly for providing me with preliminary bibliographies for McCabe and Jordan respectively. I also benefited from conversations with Paul Bew, Tony Crowley, Philip Durkin, Luke Gibbons, Jennifer Keating, Marcia Landy, Patrick Maum, Fergus Mac Cabe and Rod Stoneman.

Finally I must thank Gráinne Humphreys and Keith Hopper for the initial commission and for their kindness, a familiar Irish virtue, and patience, a most unfamiliar one, as I missed deadline after deadline. Both were invaluable sources of information about Irish cinema. Keith Hopper and the series reader for Cork University Press, Seán Ryder, improved the final text very considerably.

Pittsburgh, 9 February 2006

The editors would also like to thank Desiree Finnegan, Julie Heath, Warner Bros. Entertainment, Mark Mulqueen, Marcus McDonald, Orna Roche, and the Irish Film Institute. A special thank you to Caroline Somers and Sara Wilbourne.

1

A TALE OUT OF MONAGHAN

I first saw *The Butcher Boy* in March 1998 in London when my mother asked to see it for her birthday. I was already a great admirer of Neil Jordan's work, but nothing prepared me for the power of this most Irish of films. As the extraordinary montage of grim realism and hilarious comedy, of popular culture and hallucinatory visions, unreeled to the compelling tones of Stephen Rea and Eamonn Owens performing the music of Irish–English, I felt that Ireland itself was being dramatized. Francie Brady's story is peculiarly individual, but its tale of mania and murder, of class and religion, figures allegorically the terrible impasses that made the state that gained its partial independence in 1922 a byword for bigotry and repression. However, the strength and power of the film is not to be limited to a political history of constitutions and treaties. Indeed, the film guys a society in which everyone and his brother was best friends with Michael Collins or Eamon de Valera and where the bitter Irish Civil War of 1922–23 was both perpetually remembered and completely forgotten. *The Butcher Boy* reaches much deeper into the realities of rural Ireland to a world where death is as close as the local slaughterhouse.

Indeed the great novel on which Jordan's film was based had one of its narrative origins in a famous murder trial. The writer Patrick McCabe remembers hearing a radio play, *He Lies in Armagh Jail* by Patrick Shay, which recounted a notorious Clones murder of 1902. Two young friends, one working in a slaughterhouse and one selling chickens and eggs, met up after the poultry merchant had had a spectacularly successful day. He was never seen again. Nine months later the local RIC sergeant told the slaughterhouseman that the manure at the back of his slaughterhouse constituted a health hazard and had to be cleared. When the two young lads who had been given the job started digging, they immediately unearthed a human leg in a boot. The poultry merchant's body, having been butchered like a pig, had been covered in quicklime, but the quicklime had not in fact dissolved the body. The slaughterhouseman protested his innocence and it was only after three trials that he was brought to the gallows, where he confessed his guilt for a crime which had apparently been sparked by a demand for the return of a small loan.

The way in which this story illuminated the realities of rural Ireland inspired Patrick McCabe as he sat down to begin a new novel in the late 1980s. McCabe had been writing in a disciplined way for nearly two decades, but he had also pursued the profession of primary school teacher as a conscientious husband and father determined to ensure economic stability for himself and his family. While beginning this most solid of careers, he had also played semi-professional country-and-western music in the pubs and clubs of central Ireland and consumed, if his novels are to be believed, industrial quantities of hallucinogens before a move to a teaching job in a London primary school led to a more full-time commitment to the written word.

Monaghan

McCabe was born into a family of five in the town of Clones in County Monaghan. Monaghan is an inland county situated in the north midlands of Ireland. It was one of the three counties of the historic region of Ulster, which was judged too Catholic to be included in the Protestant statelet of Northern Ireland in the negotiations which led to the partition of the island in 1922 and the establishment of the Irish Free State. Indeed, Monaghan has some claim to be one of the most Irish of counties. In the first wave of English invasions, which followed upon the Anglo-Norman king Henry II obtaining a papal bull which granted him the country of Ireland from the only Englishman ever to sit on the throne of St Peter, Nicholas Breakspeare, Monaghan remained outside Anglo-Norman domination. Indeed, it may have been to resist such domination that the McCabes, a clan from the south-west of Scotland, made the brief journey which separates the counties of Ayrshire and Antrim. This is a journey which has carried men and women back and forth between tribe and family for more than 5,000 years and which survived the disappearance of the land bridge that linked the two countries. The McCabes probably came as Gaelic-speaking mercenaries, fighting alongside their fellow Gaelic speakers against the French-speaking Anglo-Normans, who never gained the ascendancy in Monaghan that they were to enjoy in much of the rest of Ireland.

Ireland was, however, to suffer much more terrible and bloody invasions in the sixteenth and seventeenth centuries. First the Elizabethan aristocrats and their lackeys attempted to impose themselves as the local landowning class. The bitterness and viciousness of this fight over wealth led to English fantasies of genocide. If one reads Edmund Spenser's *The Faerie Queene* (1590–96), one inhabits an imaginary vast and fertile landscape practically without native inhabitants. There is no doubt that one real vast and fertile landscape that Spenser wished to inhabit without its native inhabitants was Ireland. Spenser had been granted land in Ireland as a reward for his services to the Leicester family but his Irish idyll was interrupted by one of the savage risings through which the native people manifested their rage at the theft of both land and way of life. Spenser's house was burnt and he had to flee. The 1590s were punctuated by such risings and the Irish wars consumed Englishmen and their reputations on a terrifying scale throughout that period. Spenser penned a pamphlet on the current state of Ireland and concluded it with a call for a policy of mass starvation, much more effective than engaging in battle with the bellicose Irish:

> The proof whereof I saw sufficiently ensampled in those late wars of Munster, for notwithstanding that the same was a most rich and plentiful country, full of corn and cattle, that

3

you would have thought they would have been able to stand long, yet ere one year and a half they were brought to such wretchedness, as that any stony heart would have rued the same. Out of every corner of the woods and glens they came creeping forth upon their hands, for their legs could not bear them. They looked like anatomies of death, they spake like ghosts crying out of their graves, they did eat of the dead carrions, happy where they could find them, yea and one another soon after in so much as the very carcasses they spared not to scrape out of their graves, and if they found a plot of water cress or shamrocks, there they flocked as to a feast for the time, yet not able long to continue therewithal, that in short space there were none almost left and a most populous and plentiful country suddenly left void of man or beast. Yet sure in all that war there perished not many by the sword, but all by the extremity of famine, which they themselves had wrought.[1]

For all the efforts of the Tudor State, Ireland remained outside the detailed political control of England well into the seventeenth century. Such a state of affairs could not survive the establishment of a free commonwealth in England. When Cromwell determined to finish with 'that man of blood' and executed Charles I on 30 January 1649, he made haste to move with his New Model Army to Ireland. A nation still strongly Catholic and with potential links to the Catholic monarchies of France and Spain was as intolerable politically and militarily to the regicides as it was unacceptable to men who believed that every Christian should determine his own faith through a careful reading of the Bible. Cromwell's terror campaign in the autumn of 1649 was of a savagery which is partially explained by the real threat that Ireland posed to a Protestant English state. It was not until the first half of the nineteenth century, when famine and emigration had decimated the Irish and industrialization had prompted a population explosion in England, that Ireland ceased to be a potential military threat to England.

Cromwell's solution to that threat was not simply military terror but to pursue much more vigorously the policy of plantation. Plantation went much further than imposing an English landowner to exploit the Irish farmer's surplus: now English and Scottish farmers, Protestant and loyal to the English state, replaced the indigenous Catholics. Ulster was particularly targeted, both because of its geographical proximity to Scotland but also because it had been the most recalcitrant and rebellious of Ireland's four provinces. Monaghan, unlike most of Ulster, escaped this fate, as it had escaped the Anglo-Normans, but the result three hundred years later was that those who wished to remain a part of a Protestant state had no wish to retain a predominantly Catholic county. Although McCabe's parents were to settle in Monaghan, both came from the other side of the new border, his father from Belfast and his mother, a Maguire (a dominant clan in the county of Fermanagh), from Tyrone.

A Second Spain

His parents were to grow up in the newly independent Ireland created by the blood sacrifice of the Easter Rising, Michael Collins's terror campaign and de Valera's Catholic nationalist ideology. That ideology was elaborated on the assumption that Ireland would evade the perils of modernity by returning to its Gaelic past unsullied by the modernizing English. The power of this vision is powerfully articulated in the monstrous final stanza of Yeats' 1938 poem 'The Statues':

> When Pearse summoned Cuchulain to his side,
> What stalked through the Post Office? What intellect,
> What calculation, number, measurement, replied?
> We Irish, born into that ancient sect
> But thrown upon the filthy modern tide

> And by its formless, spawning, fury wrecked,
> Climb to our proper dark. . . .[2]

The Irish 'proper dark', like the society of the Sharia law or the Cambodian Year Zero, had nothing but an imaginary existence. If you went back beyond the invading English, all you found were the invading Vikings. However, from the Gaelic revival on, from Pearse to Bin Laden, the most powerful political appeal on the planet is to a pure historical past which will right the terrible injustices and cruelties of the present. It may seem that these comparisons are very unjust to Pearse, a democrat who founded a European state which was to maintain its democratic constitution through the twenties and thirties when the siren calls of fascism and military dictatorship found ready audiences across Europe. However, it is important to recognize that the ideology of a return to an imaginary and alternative past, which was at the centre of Pearse's vision, was to prove the most powerful political ideology that the world has known. If, in the half century after 1916, it might have seemed that the global slogans of the Bolshevik revolution of 1917 dwarfed the parochial appeals of the nationalist rising, it has been clear since Khomeini's revolution in Iran that the emotional force of the appeal to a form of community untouched by modernity and guaranteed by the past is, in fact, the most pressing political reality of our time and it is Pearse rather than Lenin who seems the more prescient political leader.[3]

The real effect of this appeal to an imaginary Irish identity was the total domination of the Catholic Church in every aspect of Irish cultural and social life. When before World War I the repulsive Carson had threatened armed revolt in Ulster to prevent Ireland gaining the measure of autonomy promised by the proposal of Home Rule, his most powerful slogan was 'Home Rule is Rome Rule'. The awful reality was that the slogan's power lay in its truth. James Joyce, living in exile in Paris in the twenties and determined never to return to the country that had made him, put it at its most succinct:

In the Dublin of my day there was the kind of desperate freedom which comes from a lack of responsibility for the English were in governance then, so everyone said what he liked. Now I hear that since the Free State came in there is less freedom. The Church has made inroads everywhere, so that we are in fact becoming a bourgeois nation, with the Church supplying the aristocracy . . . and I do not see much hope for us intellectually. Once the Church is in command she will devour everything; what she will leave will be a few old rags not worth the having: and we may degenerate to the position of a second Spain.[4]

Early Novels: *Music on Clinton Street* and *Carn*

It was into this second Spain that Patrick McCabe was born in 1955, but the sixties were to see the 'proper dark' of the de Valeran State overwhelmed by the 'filthy tide' of modernity. McCabe's first novel, *Music on Clinton Street* (1986), takes this conflict at its most acute in opposing the world of sex and drugs and rock 'n' roll of the late sixties to the Maynooth Catholicism which had dominated Irish life from the time of Catholic emancipation. After the Cromwellian settlement and through the eighteenth century and the union of the two kingdoms in 1800, Irish Catholics suffered a discrimination as savage and as prolonged as can be imagined. This discrimination included exclusion from all the political and educational institutions of the country and continuous attack on the Irish systems of land tenure. The only recourse the Irish had was violence: the failed rising of the United Irishmen and the endless secret societies of 'White Boys' and 'Ribbonmen' in which the Irish peasant defended his land not in a court by day but by cut throats and butchered animals at night. However, by 1829 Sir Robert Peel had finally yielded to the enormous pressure for Catholic emancipation and the Irish had obtained the right to practise legally the Catholic faith.

Most importantly, they could begin to construct their own educational system, a system dominated by the seminary, which from 1795 had provided training for Irish priests. Maynooth is a name which echoes down the following century and more. The product of a post-Tridentine Catholic Church which had absorbed all the more repressive aspects of Protestantism, and terrified of the anti-clericalism which had animated the French revolution and all those who took their inspiration from the slogan of 'Liberty, Equality and Fraternity', Maynooth Catholicism has some claim to be one of the most miserable forms of Christianity ever to have darkened the planet. It was to darken Ireland for well over a hundred years, its grip inexorably tightening when, with the advent of independence, and in accord with Carson's prediction, the state and the Catholic Church effectively became one. McCabe dramatizes the power of this Church and its almost exclusive focus on the 'one sin' of sex in a heart-breaking scene in his second novel, *Carn* (1989). Josie Kernan, having been abused by her father and having had to kill her illegitimate child, finally escapes from the nuns who hold her in one of the institutions that will figure so centrally in *The Butcher Boy*. Happening upon on old farmer, she introduces him to erotic joys that have been denied him all his life. But even in the deepest countryside Josie cannot escape the reach of the Church. A priest and a nun track her down and, assuming all the powers of the state without reference either to the police or the law (indeed, Josie has committed no crime), re-imprison her in a convent.

To attack Maynooth now is a bit like preaching against sin. An institution which dictated the morals and conduct of a country for nearly two centuries is now just another establishment of tertiary education. Indeed, the classic attack on the power of its narrow and terrifying vision of life antedated by nearly a decade that vision's assumption of state power. The refusal to obey Maynooth's repression of both art and desire form the major subject matter of James Joyce's *A Portrait of the Artist as a Young Man* (1916) and explain clearly why, for Joyce, the national liberation of 1922 was a hollow sham so dangerous that he would never return to the country of his birth and would spend the rest of his life writing an alternative version of Irish freedom in *Finnegans Wake* (1939).

McCabe's loathing of Maynooth is clear enough throughout his work, but *Music on Clinton Street* makes clear it is a loathing informed by a very considerable sympathy. The second chapter of this first novel throws a historical eye on the way that, in the wake of emancipation, and resisting Peel's attempt to establish non-denominational education, the Catholic hierarchy harnessed a subject race's pride to construct a national system of Catholic schooling. The focus is local: the efforts of Joe Kilgannon to find the land and money to build St Xavier's Diocesan College in a 'bit of Ulster's rump'. The mixing of the religious and the national is constant:

In the days when the poor people of Ireland were rambling the roads in search of a good field of nettles or scoffing their stirabout behind the grey walls of the workhouse, a learned man in a black soutane stood on a hillside and said to himself: 'We haven't enough men to lead this crowd off their knees and out of the ditch. We'll have to get ourselves a place' . . . Joe knew them their seed and breed. Watched them battle the one acre scrub, those who had nothing but their tattered rags on their backs, who had waited nightly for the battering of the militia on the half door. And he knew that if he could get the money he needed he could give them something. For too long the tall erect figure of the alien had strolled among the trees with his guards, ever vigilant for the darting eyes of a native in the shadows. Food was alright but to look him full square in the teeth, more was needed and Joe knew. God and the Greeks and Ovid. Then they'd crawl from their prison, the triumphant glare of the planter would not bend them. They would build their own ikons . . . Every

9

man gave a half penny or a chicken or a clutch of eggs. (*Music on Clinton Street*, pp. 15–17)

Joe Kilgannon builds his college and the elite of the oppressed Catholics funnel all their energies into entering the priesthood, creating the foundations for the celibate and ultra-masculine aristocracy that Joyce so feared. The key year for St Xavier's in McCabe's narrative is 1919. In that year, the English realize the game is up: 'the walrus moustache men decided it was time to start selling the drapes and the French paintings and buy their ticket for the boat, for the ragged woman with the creel of junk outside the boarded up cottage had pointed the bone at them and they knew it' (*Music on Clinton Street*, p. 22).

Just as important, that year sees the arrival of electricity and the huge Victorian buildings that dot the countryside, as the huge Victorian churches decorate the towns, are suddenly illuminated by electricity from within, as they will three years later be authorized by a Catholic state from without. They become those 'buildings with a hundred windows' shining in the night in which two generations of the Bradys will be humiliated and abused. In *The Butcher Boy* the focus will be on the reform schools and the lunatic asylums, but the first model for these Maynooth houses of pain is St Xavier's diocesan college in *Music on Clinton Street*, clearly modelled on the school that McCabe himself attended from the age of twelve and of which he has nothing but the most dismal memories: 'nothing but football and rain'.

What is interesting about *Music on Clinton Street* is that while the ostensible hero of the novel is young Des, exactly the same age as McCabe when he started secondary school, the sympathetic centre of the text is Philip the Junior Dean, a young priest formed in the tradition of Maynooth and unwilling to adopt the trendy compromises which the sixties are forcing on the Catholic Church.

McCabe's greatest strength as a writer is his ability to weave objective description and subjective hallucination into a compelling world. This is the fundamental form in *The Butcher Boy*, but in the earlier novels such passages only flicker through much more conventional narrative structures. One such powerful passage in *Music on Clinton Street* comes when Philip drinks himself into a stupor as he contemplates his subterranean feud with the senior dean Vin, a guitar-playing modernizer. As the whiskey takes hold, Philip invokes the shade of the founder Joe Kilgannon, but when Joe speaks he can only confirm what Philip already knows: that the old order is dead and buried. 'The days of brittle women rattling death-prayers in the front row, bony fingers crawling towards the oblong emptiness with each bead they passed' has vanished (*Music on Clinton Street*, p. 60). The strength of McCabe's vision, and its uncompromising realism, is that while he clearly sees the terrible limitations of the old order, he has no faith whatsoever in the consumerism which is set to replace it as the 'brittle women' move into their bungalows and golf clubs. Indeed it is impossible to understand McCabe's universe without recognizing that his attacks on the repressive insularity of the de Valeran polity are all the more violent because he has understood the appeal of that vision of an Ireland insulated from the terrors of modernity.

The first cracks in the theocratic state established in 1922 come in 1959 when de Valera retires from the Premiership and Seán Lemass takes power on a programme of attracting international investment. Although tangential to *The Butcher Boy*, this economic transformation of the sixties is one of McCabe's major themes in both *Carn* and his later novel, *Call Me The Breeze* (2003). Indeed the Butcher Boy, Francie Brady, is a major character in *Carn* under the alternative name of James Cooney and in a different parallel universe where he has emigrated to America and comes back to Ireland, enticed by Lemass's policies, to buy up the town: 'It was not long before the citizens of Carn began to notice the imposing figure of James Cooney. They remembered him as a quiet retiring youth who had worn his brother's trousers three sizes too big for him and carted offal from the abattoir in a zinc bucket' (*Carn*, p. 12). James Cooney testifies to the fertility of McCabe's imagination and the protean quality of his imaginary town of Carn, which shares the geographical position and historical features of his own home town of Clones. It also enables us to avoid any simple concept of realism when analysing the power of McCabe's writing. That his imaginative world is rooted in the small town of Clones is indubitable. It is to be read in every novel; McCabe himself stresses it in every interview; it is remarked in every intelligent review. However, it would be the greatest folly to think that McCabe's work offers us a simple representation of his home town or of his own life. If one were looking for a parallel, one would have to find it in William Faulkner. It is not simply that the imaginary county Yoknapatawpha is the most illuminating parallel for the imaginary town of Carn, but Faulkner's style – blending subjective vision with objective fact in prose whose rhythms merge both spoken and written – is very close to McCabe's. Traditional accounts of realism falter because they operate a divorce between representation and world which fails to understand how both are part of each other. The realist novel normally does little more than repeat already established structures of representation, finding content for an already established form. It is not a reflection of the world, but a key element in its repetition. Novels which really seek new content find new forms which produce contents that break this repetition, fracturing the general social and political development in unpredictable ways. Faulkner's novels made the South readable in new ways, ways which become part of the transformations of America in the fifties and sixties. McCabe's *The Butcher Boy* found a form in which he could finally allow the heterogeneity of his experience to sing into life the town in which his social imagination had been formed. The consequences of the creation of Francie Brady is to add substantially to the reality of Ireland. It is not that the Francie Bradys of this world lacked existence nor even that they did not figure in the tables of juvenile delinquency and truant children. What McCabe's novel does is to allow the reader a very different access to this existence, an access which it is quite reasonable to describe as the production of a new social reality. Francie Brady draws much from McCabe's own childhood, although the fact that Francie is an only child and McCabe had four brothers and sisters should immediately caution against any simple equation of author and protagonist. Similarly, McCabe's own family never plumbed the social depths of the Bradys. There also can be little doubt that the imaginative feat that brings Francie to life has much to do with McCabe's experience as a teacher. Finding himself increasingly at odds with school authorities, McCabe opted early on to teach children with learning difficulties, where he could teach as he wished. It is tempting to think that his ability to empathize with his charges owed something to a lifestyle which often operated on the margins of society and where the intensity of hallucinogenic experiences made the boundaries between normal and abnormal less obvious.

Both McCabe's first and second novels take the experience of small-town Ireland in the sixties as their starting-point but the second novel, *Carn*, brings the story up to the present, interweaving the sexual repressions of Maynooth Catholicism and the advent of the international culture of sex, drugs and rock 'n' roll with the history of Irish republicanism as the apparent calm of the sixties is followed by the outbreak of a full-scale guerrilla war across the border. *Carn* is a very considerable novel in its own right, but in some ways it marks a step back from *Music on Clinton Street*, which in its most powerful passages abandoned a third-person narrative structure to plunge into a blending of first- and third-person, for which indirect free style would be far too anaemic a formal description. *Carn*, although full of remarkable passages where description and consciousness fuse, is, in its attempt to encompass all the different elements of the town, positively George Eliot-like in the omniscient position it grants both writer and reader. The result is, despite McCabe's valiant efforts, an inevitable feeling of superiority to the limited repertoire of pleasures and pains enjoyed by the inhabitants of Carn.

The Ur-text: 'Baby Pig'

When McCabe sat down to write his next novel he was determined to 'find a style that suited my soul'. And there is no doubt that the soul was intensely local. Quizzed as to whether he ever had the ambition to be the Great Irish Novelist, McCabe insists that no such thought ever entered his mind, but he does confess to a desire to be the great Clones novelist. He stresses that he was always convinced that 'If I could get this place right then everything else would flow'.

His third novel was an attempt to get this place right. It marks a decisive break with the earlier writing and coincides with McCabe's move to England. There is no doubt that 'Baby Pig', the draft manuscript of *The Butcher Boy*, signals the moment at which writing became McCabe's central imaginative occupation. As in *Music in Clinton Street*, we see events from the perspective of an adolescent but the trio of the Captain, Matthew and the father are no longer pillars of the community full of reminiscences of their youth or, rather, they are such pillars full of such reminiscences but the difference of perspective is stark from the opening pages. Des, the curiously anonymous and passive youth of *Music on Clinton Street*, is replaced by Francie Brady. This Francie starts the novel well outside the law, living a feral existence in the ruined railway station where he spies the Captain making love to a young girl from the year above him in school:

> It was hard to believe that The Captain got up to those things with her. I had known him for years from him coming around to the house to talk football with the old man and Matthew. He'd show me his championship medals. *Ah yes, that was the year we beat Cork*, he'd say. ('Baby Pig', p. 5)

But the transformation of the Captain is as nothing to what happens to Matthew and the father. Matthew, the schoolteacher, collapses into drunken despair after his wife Ann Marie leaves him. Indeed it is the fantasy of Matthew and Ann Marie's happiness in the early days of their marriage and their time at the seaside resort of Bundoran that obsesses Francie in this early version of the Brady story. Francie's mother appears both in the fight over the comics with Mrs Nugent and at Alo's party, but she is largely an absent figure confined to a mental home. The father is an alcoholic who has reached stages of addiction that are only hinted at in *The Butcher Boy*. In a scene after Mrs Nugent has called Da Brady a pig, he is escorted home from the pub, his mouth flecked with vomit and his trousers soiled. Mrs Nugent, who in this book's geography lives next to the Bradys, revels in the sight:

> She didn't say anything. She was going to speak when she was ready and not before. There wasn't an inch of Da Brady but her eyes drank in. ('Baby Pig', p. 45)

Francie's revenge, breaking into the Nugents' house and soiling the clothes in Mrs Nugent's chest of drawers, causes Mrs Nugent to leave town early in the book, having suffered a nervous breakdown and with her marriage ruined. It also causes a rift between Francie and Joe (called Joe Pop Purcell in this version) which will haunt them down to their last fatal encounter.

All pretence at third-person narration has been abandoned in this book and the consciousness that we inhabit is that of the eponymous and drug-fuelled narrator, Baby Pig (Francie Brady). Unlike *The Butcher Boy*, however, this Brady narration is episodic, flashing backwards and forwards, with key details buried within scenes far removed from their narrative origin. Thus, although Baby Pig returns to the empty Nugent house early in the book, it is not until his final conversation with Joe that we really learn what happened to the Nugents. The Francie Brady who relates this story is not the irrepressible child who dominates the first two-thirds of the published novel, but a hideous development of the violent and frightening social reject that emerges right at the end of the book we know. The perspective is completely solitary. Francie's only companion is his mongrel dog Grouse, who in one of the unpublished novel's many brutal scenes has his throat cut by the gang of youths (called the Park Street boys) who constantly attack and humiliate Francie.

The change of form brings immediate benefits at the level of the writing: there are descriptive passages of great intensity and many of the themes of *The Butcher Boy* find eloquent expression. It is, however, hardly surprising that 'Baby Pig' was rejected by the publisher Aidan Ellis, who had been one of McCabe's staunchest supporters. It is only comprehensible as a narrative if one reads it in the light of *Music on Clinton Street* and *The Butcher Boy*. Indeed, it is hard to quarrel with Ellis's judgement that the book needed a great deal of editing. Scene after scene, however, illuminate the published novel considerably. One of the most striking is a much extended account of the introduction of the Brady brothers into the home which so haunts Francie's father. In the published work it is a short paragraph as Francie runs away from home after the catastrophic end to Alo's party:

> I kept thinking of da and Alo standing outside the gates of the home all those years ago. How many windows do you think are there says da. Seventy five says Alo. I'd say at least a hundred says da. The priest brought them inside through long polished corridors. The assembly hall was crowded. They were all cheering for the two new boys. The priest cleared his throat and said quiet please. I would like you to meet our two new boys he said. Bernard and Alo. Bernard and Alo who? said all the other boys. The priest smiled and rubbed his soft hands together. I was waiting for him to say *Brady* and finish it. But he didn't say Brady. He said: Pig. (*The Butcher Boy*, p. 39)

In the unpublished ur-novel the scene occupies some six pages, providing a great deal of detailed background on the behaviour of Andy Brady, who had drunk away 'a thriving grocery and off-licence business' and put his wife into a mental hospital. The whole scene is orchestrated by the sadistic priest as a prolonged question-and-answer sequence in which the priest eggs his audience on to find the description that fits the behaviour of the father of the two humiliated children standing before them. It is typical of the fantastic world of the book that Francie finds himself in the audience desperate to answer the priest's questions:

Out of nowhere I was there. I was the man to answer that one. Up went my hand like a shot.

'Well well, look who it is, young Francie,' smiled the priest. 'So you think you know the answer, do you Francie? Right let's hear it!'

I stammered a bit with all the excitement but I got my tongue around the words all right.

'Not a man Father,' I said, 'Not a man at all.'

'Yes!' said the priest, reeling me in like a pike, 'Yes?'

He was balancing on one leg as he cocked his ear.

'*A Pig!*' I cried out.

'*Absolutely correct,*' cried the priest.

He was over the moon. You could see it. He clapped. Then everybody clapped. They all gave me the thumbs up.

'Fair play to you Francie!' the priest cried, 'that was an excellent answer. Full marks to Francis there!'

'Well done, Francie! Not many people are lucky enough to have a pig as a grandfather!'

I was hot and flushed and excited and I couldn't be stopped.

'No no you don't understand,' I said, 'There's more!'

The priest stood back.

'More?' he exclaimed, 'Are you sure Francis?'

'Yes,' I called out breathlessly, 'Da Brady here turned out to be a pig as well!' The priest gasped. He fell back stunned by this revelation.

'Well boys oh boys,' he cried, producing a sheet of a hankie from the depth of his pocket like a magician and starting to dab his forehead, '*Now who would ever have thought that!*'

He was only acting the jackass with me but I was so excited and fired up that I didn't see that.

'No!' He cried again in mock amazement, 'You're trying to make a cod out of me Francis!'

'No Father, I'm not. I swear it's true! If you don't believe me look outside The Step Down Inn any night and you'll see! If you think the grandfather was bad you should see him! He's the King of the Pigs! It's true! I'm telling you!' ('Baby Pig', pp. 56–7)

The identification of the Bradys with the pigs, so striking in the novel, is thus made even more explicit in the ur-text (indeed it provides the title of the unpublished novel). The emphasis here is on the pig as the image of the uncivilized, the fair-skinned animal of roughly human size who shares with the human species an omnivorous diet and many other biological characteristics but whose very similarity to man makes him the symbol of the not human. To call someone sheepish is hardly complimentary and to call a woman a cow or a bitch is deeply insulting, but it is only the pig (and its cognates 'hog' and 'swine') whose very name suggests behaviour in which animal appetite has triumphed over civilized manners. The depth of this identification can be measured by the fact that these connotations are general throughout all the European languages. Of course, this general human imagery has a particular history in an Ireland where the English estimation of the Irish as sub-human has summoned forth a host of animal imagery, of which in the late nineteenth and early twentieth century the dominant figure was the pig. In particular, the Irishman was frequently depicted as living with his pig and Flann O'Brien's widely praised Gaelic novel, *An Beal Bocht* (1941) (translated as *The Poor Mouth*, 1973), gains much of its comedy by playing on the stereotype of Paddy and his pig sharing living quarters.[5]

This stereotype itself finds some of its force in the grinding poverty of the Irish peasantry, in which a cow represented riches beyond the dreams of avarice and a pig might indeed be a family's most important economic asset.[6] In McCabe's world of post-independence Ireland, the pig becomes the dominating metaphor for class division. Francie Brady, whose father finds employment as a stonemason, lives in the same street as Joe Pop Purcell, the vet's son, and the impeccably bourgeois Nugents. When Mrs Nugent comes round to complain about the theft of her son's comics, she is explicit that in behaving like pigs they are conforming to a racial stereotype:

> I don't suppose you could expect much else from a house where the father's never out of the pub and treats his wife like a pig. Maybe we should have stayed in England where people have some respect for themselves. (McCabe, 'Baby Pig', p. 40)

It would be conventional to analyse this position in terms of a post-colonial consciousness in which the dominant terms of the imperialist oppressor have been internalized and in which deep shame attaches to membership of a subject race. The problem with almost all post-colonial analyses is that they remain tied to a notion of political correctness in which it would be possible to find the ideal psychic and political form with which to throw off both the shame of colonial subjugation and the political inheritance of imperialism.

McCabe's concern was not with ideal forms but in allowing a set of *emotions* – emotions connected to the real shame of Irish drunkenness and mania, to the impoverished sexual and emotional lives of the post-independence generation of his parents – to find voice. Aidan Ellis's rejection went deep and led to what McCabe himself calls 'a dark night of the soul'. He remembers clearly coming back to a holiday in Ireland secure in his job and happy with his family but feeling that he had reached an absolute dead end. On returning to England he sat down to wrestle once again with the material that had obsessed him for twenty years. In a few short months he wrote *The Butcher Boy*.

2

THE NOVEL

The Narrative

McCabe himself is insistent that there was no question of intellectual reflection; that the new story of Francie Brady was not the result of an analysis of the previous text's weaknesses. For McCabe it was a question of tapping emotional levels which had not yet found voice. What can clearly be said, however, is that McCabe drastically simplified his narrative and it is this simpler narrative structure that is the spine of both novel and film. Out go Matthew and the Captain, with the different perspectives they offer on the previous generation, out go the large cast of Francie's contemporaries (the Park Street boys, Monkey, Bridie) and the complicated levels of class and sexual rivalry which they represent. Just as important, the episodic style of the novel is abandoned for a simple frame within which the story of Francie Brady is told chronologically. Francie grows up within a tragically dysfunctional family, his father a chronic alcoholic and his mother a suicidal manic-depressive. Francie's most valued relationship is with his friend Joe Purcell, with whom he plays elaborate games which draw on the popular culture of comics, film and, perhaps most importantly, the television (new to Ireland in 1962). After a party in honour of Benny Brady's brother, Alo, home for a visit from England, Francie's parents explode into a particularly violent row. Fleeing the row, Francie runs away to Dublin and on his return finds that his mother has committed suicide. Francie's world now becomes increasingly focused on the Nugents, whose son Philip represents a rival for Joe's affections and whose bourgeois bliss constitutes a temptation to disown his own inadequate parents. His first assault on the Nugents (as in 'Baby Pig') is to invade their house and to assert his animal identity in the most evident fashion. For this repellent schoolboy prank he is sent away to an industrial school, where he is sexually abused by a priest. The Irish industrial schools were the result of a system that saw the social provisions of the Victorian British state entirely delivered into the hands of the Catholic Church. Francie's via dolorosa takes him through the belly of the beast of the de Valeran state.[7]

Back in the town but unable to continue with his education he takes a job at the local slaughterhouse. His efforts to constitute a normal home now become truly demented as he refuses to recognize that his father has died and keeps his body at home, the centre of domestic bliss. By the time the police and the doctor break into the house, the father's body is full of maggots and Francie is taken away for a second time but this time to a mental home rather than an industrial school. When he returns to the town for a second time, Philip and Joe inhabit a different teenage world and are both at a nearby boarding school.

The final act of the narrative witnesses Francie's increasingly disturbed and violent behaviour. Desperate to confirm his long-cherished image of his parents' honeymoon as a moment of genuine romantic bliss, Francie travels to the seaside town of Bundoran to track down the boarding-house where they stayed. The landlady unfortunately does remember Francie's parents: she remembers Benny Brady drunk on his own honeymoon behaving like a pig to his wife. Francie's final attempt to connect with a human world takes him to Joe's school in the middle of the night, where, having woken both pupils and staff, he is finally rejected by Joe. For Francie this final betrayal focuses his paranoid fantasies on Mrs Nugent. He returns to the town where the Cuban missile crisis has provoked a collective belief that Our Lady is about to appear and bring a miraculous peace to the world. Francie's miracle is to kill Mrs Nugent and gut her like a pig with tools he takes from the slaughterhouse.

In the climax of the aftermath of Mrs Nugent's murder Francie attempts to commit suicide by burning down his house and all the memories in it. He is rescued from the conflagration and confined to the mental home from which he has told us his story.

This summary is accurate but is about as far from the tone and spirit of the book as it is possible to get. The book's astonishing feat is to relate this story from Francie's point of view and to make it richly comic and fundamentally ecstatic. The single most important element in this feat is the language of Francie's voice, a voice which, in comparison to 'Baby Pig', has thrown off the need to provide levels of novelistic description in favour of a continuous focus on language as an instrument of emotion. This difference can be read in many of the passages which the ur-novel and the published book share, such as, for example, the scene in the Belfast boys' home, but nowhere is it clearer than in the scene which functions as Francie's touchstone of happiness – his first meeting with Joe.

In 'Baby Pig', this meeting which formally prefaces Francie's account of his own life is full of the kind of detail which we associate with the traditional realist novel. Joe sitting by the puddle hacking at the ice is described both in terms of his clothes and his surroundings. Although the voice is Francie's the perspective is still that of the novelist. In *The Butcher Boy*, all such peripheral concerns are gone – we see Joe from Francie's point of view, undisturbed by any traditional novelistic description. As a result its emotional core, its role as the one sure example of happiness in a life beset by disappointment and betrayal, is magnified – its reality attested to by its place in Francie's fantasies. This is not to suggest that McCabe's craft as a novelist is not at work, indeed the narrative is both simpler, with a clear chronological organization, and more complex, with the introduction of both the industrial school and the mental asylum. To take one minor example, Francie no longer lives next to the Nugents and the Purcells and this geographical relocation makes much clearer the class differences so crucial in the destruction of Francie's world. But we deduce such differences from the development of Francie's story – a story entirely written in the language of Monaghan.

Irish English

Both McCabe and Jordan place great emphasis on the authenticity of language in book and film (perhaps the single most important feature of the film qua film is that it harnessed a budget from a Hollywood studio to a dialogue track which privileged native speakers over international audiences) and both describe the language as 'Elizabethan'. It is certainly the case that the English spoken in Ireland derives from Elizabethan English in a more important way than British English, for there is no significant record of English being spoken in Ireland before that period. It is also the case that Irish English shows a much greater degree of free variation than modern British English which was policed into being by the grammars, dictionaries and elocution manuals of the eighteenth century. But what Jordan and McCabe are referring to is a joy and pleasure in a language and its possibilities which is difficult to square with conventional histories.

From early in the Anglo-Norman conquest, there is a frequent complaint about the conquerors going native and adopting the Irish language and customs. This complaint becomes policy in the seventeenth century, where abjuring Catholicism and abandoning Irish were equivalent in many English Protestant minds. Cromwell's second parliament passed an Act against Popish recusants, which required suspected Catholics to take an oath which *inter alia* denied transubstantiation and committed them to teaching their children only to speak English.[8]

Throughout the eighteenth century, Irish was discriminated against. This process culminated early in the nineteenth century with a complete remapping of Ireland with English place-names, and the early introduction of compulsory education in English testified to the British state's commitment to eradicating the Irish language as an element in rendering Ireland an obedient member of the body politic.[9]

The trouble with this history is that it in no way explains why the vast majority of Irish speakers abandoned their mother tongue. Similar histories in countries as close as Wales yield very different results. Indeed it is not clear that any historical parallel exists for a people so thoroughly abandoning their own language. Many find an explanation in the Famine, when death and emigration more than decimated Ireland, but the problem with this hypothesis is that Irish had been abandoned long before in many parts of the country.

One such area was Monaghan, where, despite the predominance of Catholics and the lack of a planter population, there is little evidence of Irish being spoken after the late eighteenth century.[10] One clear explanation is utility – Daniel O'Connell delivered his great speeches for Catholic emancipation in English, despite Irish being his domestic language, because they were addressed not simply to the Irish crowds at his meetings but also to the English newspapers which reported them. An explanation which appealed to both Wilde and Joyce but which can hardly be said to have found favour in nationalist Ireland is that English offered real pleasures of expression and, perhaps even more importantly, the possibility of superiority. Wilde famously said that 'The Saxon took our lands from us . . . but we took their language and added new beauties to it.'[11] Joyce's version is: 'The Irish, condemned to express themselves in a language not their own, have stamped on it the mark of their own genius and compete for glory with the civilized nations. This is then called English literature.'[12] From this perspective it may not be coincidence that McCabe was able to release the beauties of the speech of his home town while living and writing in London. Francie himself remarks on the superiority of Irish English to the anaemic forms of British English aped by the bourgeoisie when he reflects on Mr Nugent:

You could see by him that he had a high-up job. He had that look in his eye that said I have a high-up job. He was staring off into the distance thinking about all the high-up things he was going to do and all the people he was going to meet. I don't know if he was English but he spoke like it. He said good afternoon when everybody else said *hardy weather* or *she looks like rain*. (*The Butcher Boy*, p. 55)

The material that went into *The Butcher Boy* had, in one way or another, been with McCabe for twenty years, but the final writing was a matter of a few months. Before *The Butcher Boy* he had published in Ireland but this time he employed an agent who sold the book to Picador. It was immediately acclaimed, shortlisted for the 1992 Booker Prize and won the Aer Lingus/*Irish Times* Fiction Prize for that year.

3

AN IRISH FILMMAKER

The Butcher Boy © 1997 Geffen Pictures. Licensed by: Warner Bros Entertainment Inc. All Rights Reserved.

Plate 1. Neil Jordan on the set of The Butcher Boy, *1997.*

Neil Jordan in 1992

For many readers it was clear that this was something genuinely new and original. Amongst those readers was another Irish writer, Neil Jordan. In an eerily prescient introduction to Jordan's first collection of short stories, published in 1976, Seán O'Faoláin hails him for abandoning the 'boring old language and symbolism of rural Ireland': 'This young man's metaphors are songs like "The Crying Game", "The Tennessee Waltz", "Night in Tunisia", a boy fingering an old piano in a dance hall, the sax wailing high . . .'

Fifteen years later, in early 1992, when Jordan was editing a film he had shot with the working title of *A Soldier's Wife*, he decided at the last moment to call it *The Crying Game*. Although a miserable failure on its English release, it went on to take more money at the

27

American box office than any previous foreign film and to win an Oscar for Best Original Screenplay. When Jordan optioned *The Butcher Boy*, which he did immediately after he read the novel in 1992, he was probably the hottest director in Britain and Ireland. He was also a director whose work McCabe, a film buff from an early age, knew well and much admired.

Jordan had been born in Sligo on the west coast of Ireland in 1950, which makes him exactly the same age as Francie Brady. When he was five his father, a teacher, had accepted a job at St Patrick's teacher training college in Drumcondra, where he taught maths and philosophy of education and where in the early seventies he would have as a student a young Patrick McCabe. Jordan was brought up in Dublin and attended University College Dublin, where he read history and wrote plays. It seems obvious that Jordan is a crucial member of a generation of writers, directors and musicians determined to recast the possibilities of Irish culture both aesthetically and economically and his career coincides with a flowering of Irish art which stretches from the Field Day collective to The Pogues and U2. It is perhaps worth adding the cautionary note that Jordan himself is very opposed to this generational explanation, which for him is largely a triumph of marketing. However, there is no doubt that the seventies and eighties saw the cultural and ideological settlement of 1922 undermined by an upsurge of historical revisions and aesthetic experiments of which Jordan's film of *The Butcher Boy* might be seen as one kind of culmination. Jordan's obsession with the cinema stretches back into his youth. He remembers his favourite cinemas in Dublin and weekends in London when he would see seven or eight films. He even applied for and was accepted by the National Film School at Beaconsfield, but there was no possibility of finding the money for the fees. He was, however, to serve a remarkable if informal apprenticeship with the great British director John Boorman, who had lived in Ireland since the sixties. Boorman read *Night in Tunisia*,

Jordan's first prizewinning collection of short stories, and felt that they were deeply influenced by the cinema. The first result was a collaboration on a script, *Broken Dreams*, which never got made. Then Boorman asked him to work with him in the preparations for filming *Excalibur* (1981), which led to Jordan being credited on the finished film as Creative Associate. In this period Jordan also wrote both for television (writing four parts of a thirteen-part series on the life of Seán O'Casey) and for the cinema (*Traveller* (1981), directed by Joe Comerford). On both occasions the direction was not to his liking and he decided that, if he wanted his scripts directed as he would wish, then he would have to direct them himself.

Angel

The film he then wrote, *Angel* (1982), owes much of its narrative structure to Boorman's own *Point Blank* (1967), in which Lee Marvin sets out on an act of serial revenge. However, its setting was the dancehalls of Ulster, which Jordan knew from his time playing saxophone in bands thrown together in Dublin and willing to play anywhere to earn some money. Its context was a fresh episode of 'The Troubles', the armed conflict which pitted a new generation of Northern republicans against the British state and which had spawned a terrifying culture of violence in both Protestant and Catholic communities. It can come as no surprise to anyone who has read his short stories that *Angel* showed little interest in the politics or even the society from which the violence springs. The focus is on one man and the consequences of violence as the protagonist, played by Stephen Rea, finds himself increasingly fascinated by the mechanics of murder. Jordan says:

> I wanted to make a stripped-down thriller movie, stripped down to the bones. I wanted to make it about the way a weapon suggests its own uses, the way it takes over the central character. I wanted to make a movie that was set in this obviously real place but didn't explain its events away.

There can be no questioning the talent or the interest of this film more than a generation later, but it is the complex soundtrack and the dancehalls of smalltown Ireland which continue to compel, while the thriller element verges on the parodic.

There can be no doubt, however, that it was the thriller element which turned the film into a minor hit. It sets a clear precedent for Jordan's films, which are remarkable in their attempt to use the commercial possibilities of genre filmmaking to investigate genuinely original material. Indeed, Jordan's genius could be summarised as an ability to know instinctively how far to employ well-understood forms without compromising the integrity of the underlying material. *The Butcher Boy* may well stand as the most impressive testament to that ability, but it was there from the very first. What was also there from the first was a real sense of visual space – the camera moves across dance floors and through streets and fields with a real sense of the frame as the fundamental dramatic unit of film. This sense is almost certainly an intuitive one at root, but *Angel* undoubtedly also provided a more than useful education.

Jordan is one of the many film graduates of Channel 4. When Jeremy Isaacs was appointed Chief Executive of the new channel, he announced that ten per cent of its revenues would go into films with the explicit aim of provoking a renaissance in British cinema. One of those recruited to select the first scripts was Walter Donohue. Donohue had been a great admirer of Jordan's writing and had already tried to commission him while working first at the Royal Shakespeare Company and then at the BBC. On both occasions Jordan had said his first priority was film and when Donohue found himself working for Film Four one of the first calls he made was to Jordan, who immediately sent him *Angel*. Donohue was even more enthusiastic about the project when Jordan said that he wanted to direct it. Separately, Boorman had recommended the film to Isaacs, who was taking a very direct interest in the Channel's first film slate. There was general enthusiasm for the script at Channel 4 but a certain wariness about so novice a director. The solution was to ask Boorman to act as Executive Producer. Boorman was worried that the great cinematographer Chris Menges, whom Jordan had chosen, would overwhelm an untried director and insisted that, if Menges was making suggestions for a shot, he must always provide alternatives. It is difficult to think of a more focused way of learning the possibilities offered by the camera.

Boorman's interest in the film was more than personal. As Chairman of the new Irish Film Board, which had been set up to encourage Irish filmmaking, he had invested almost all of the annual budget in the film and thus outraged the small but vociferous Irish filmmaking community, all of whom were still waiting to make their first feature. To add insult to injury, the Film Board handed the money which they had not spent on *Angel* back to the government, on the grounds that they had not found any other worthy projects. Hell hath no fury like *ressentiment* in a small country.[13] A generation on, it is easy to forget how Jordan was vilified and demonized, but it may be an important factor both in his desire to see *The Butcher Boy* made and in his initial hesitation as to whether he was the right person to direct it.

Angel was initially destined for the very first weeks of Channel 4's schedules and there was no thought of putting the film into cinemas in England. However, a screening was arranged in a backstreet theatre during the Cannes Film Festival to see if there would be any foreign buyers interested in the film. One of those who elbowed their way into the screening was Steve Woolley, a young film buff who, on the back of his success programming The Other Cinema, had just been employed by Nik Powell to work on a new film distribution company called Palace Pictures. So impressed was Woolley by the film that he took the next plane to London to see Boorman. Boorman was only too keen for the film, still the focus of considerable resentment in Ireland, to earn some extra revenue. The problem, however, was to find the money to produce release prints and, even more important, to persuade Channel 4 to pull the film from their early schedules and allow it a theatrical window. Both these problems were solved by Ian Christie, who had also been at the Cannes screening. Christie was working for BFI distribution and was able both to find the money for the prints and to persuade Richard Attenborough, then Chairman of the BFI and deputy chairman of Channel 4, that it was Channel 4's duty to allow the film to be seen in cinemas.

Jordan thus found himself, at the age of thirty-two, not only with a film which was a hit on the art-house circuit but also linked to the most interesting and innovative young film company in Britain, and a company whose distribution arm had proved so successful that it was keen to go into production. Although there was to be acrimony over *High Spirits* (1988) and although the success of *The Crying Game* (1992) came too late to save Palace from bankruptcy,[14] the relationship with Steve Woolley was to be an almost constant feature of Jordan's films up to and beyond *The Butcher Boy*.

Adapting *The Company of Wolves*

Most immediately it found fruit in *The Company of Wolves* (1984). Jordan had met Angela Carter at a literary festival in Dublin in 1982 and they had become friends. She showed him a short radio play that she had developed from her story 'The Company of Wolves'. Jordan came up with the idea of using as a frame the grandmother telling stories to her granddaughter, which would enable them to use more of the stories in the collection *The Bloody Chamber* (1979) and produce something long enough for a feature film. Jordan really enjoyed the collaboration:

> Every day I'd come in the morning and we'd discuss things and we'd work out how it should go; she'd make me a cup of tea, and I'd take some sections to go home and write and she'd take some sections to write and then we'd come the

next morning and we'd look at what we'd written and we'd
proceed as before and it was very organized. We did it in
about two weeks. Like two surrealists – two paintings done
by four o'clock.

It is difficult to think of any director in the history of cinema who
has been as talented a novelist as Jordan; in Europe, perhaps only
Pasolini combined a successful career as a director with a continuing
commitment to the written word. Given this talent, it might seem
strange at first that so many of his works have been adaptations or
developed from other scripts (about half of his films, to date), but any
strangeness results from a naïve prejudice about adaptation and our
very inadequate understanding of what is an absolutely fundamental
cultural process. Before the eighteenth century in the Western
tradition, much art, and certainly almost all the most interesting
literary art, was adaptation. All of Shakespeare's plays bar *The Tempest*
are adaptations and even *The Tempest* finds its origins in the Bermuda
pamphlets, which detailed a contemporary story of shipwreck in the
Caribbean. Both Aeschylus and Sophocles take their subject matter
from the stock of established Greek myth. The examples multiply.

The growth of a literary market in the eighteenth century and the
branding of novelty in the form of the novel was one element in the
cultural decline of adaptation. More important, however, was the
Romantic valuation of the individual imagination and the elaboration
of our still contemporary notion of the author as the origin of artistic
creation. While that notion continues its ideological dominance,
developments in both high and popular culture counter it. In one of
the key essays of high modernism, 'Tradition and the Individual
Talent', T. S. Eliot articulated one powerful notion of an anti-
Romantic ideology in which the notion of the conscious mind as an
origin for art is ridiculed in favour of a dialectic between individual
experience, no longer identified with a conscious intentionality, and
the forms, for Eliot above all linguistic and poetic forms, which the

artist inherits. Nearly fifty years later Roland Barthes was to produce a more millenarian version of Eliot's modernism in which the 'death of the author' allowed the reader to enjoy the infinite interpretation of the codes and forms from which art is produced. Michel Foucault, in a long if implicit critique of Barthes' formulations, stressed the variety of legal, commercial and educational discourses which constituted authorship. The no less millenarian aim of Foucault was to fragment rather than to abolish the author.

What was surprising about Barthes' and Foucault's articles was that neither made any reference to cinema, given that the most important theory of authorship of the post-war era had been developed in Paris in the *Cahiers du Cinema*. However, André Bazin set up his magazine in deliberate opposition both to the university, then famously antipathetic to popular culture, and to the official discourses of the left, for whom Hollywood films were imperialist culture.[15] Romantic theories of authorship ignored both the importance of the pre-existing forms from which art was constructed and the centrality of the markets in which it was sold. *Cahiers* stressed the importance of the forms – one recognized an author exactly by his use of lighting, camera position, décor, stars – and of the business in which the author had to operate – *Cahiers* was fascinated by the politics of the Hollywood studios. If *Cahiers* continued to stress the author as individual, they had no interest in the idea of origin. Indeed the defining manifesto of the auteur theory, Truffaut's famous 'A Certain Tendancy of French Cinema', defined authorship in relation to adaptation. It was exactly the ability of a director to take a literary narrative and turn it into a cinematic narrative which defined a true filmmaker. The simple transposition of the narrative meant nothing unless the specific codes of cinema were being fully utilized. When Truffaut wrote, he was drawing on two luminous articles that André Bazin had already written on adaptation.[16] Bazin was clear that, if the filmmaker was faithful to the work, then that fidelity was the finding in the cinematic codes of patterns which extend and develop the original work.

Jordan's adaptation of Angela Carter's short stories is a feast of cinematic codes drawing on a mixture of genres and a range of actors and special effects. The single most striking element is the imaginary English village and wood which the myriad talents of the designer Anton Furst conjured into being on a Pinewood sound stage. It is on this set that the various tales of Carter's short stories get played out – their unreality grounded as a young girl's dream. When I first saw the film when it opened in London, I was astonished at Jordan's ability to find new resources to investigate the most permanent features of the human condition. If some of the symbolism was laid on with a trowel, the film constructed a coherent imaginary world in which the range and power of the images produced a genuine sense of the uncanny. The film indeed managed to evoke a real sense of the ambiguities of sexuality – the human paradox of beasts who are 'hairy on the inside'. Jordan had done something that I had thought impossible: he showed that there was genuine life in British cinema and *The Company of Wolves* intensified my own desire to work in film.

The ending of Carter's original short story has the girl asleep 'between the paws of the tender wolf'[17] and that beautiful phrase provides a classic example of the problems of adaptation. The simple visual representation of this phrase would provide something at best bizarre and at worst ludicrous. The double structure of the film gives Jordan two endings. The first, a brilliant equivalence of Carter's sentence, is a finale to Little Red Riding Hood where the girl leaps fluidly through the window to join the company of wolves. However, the very final scene of the movie take us back to the young girl's bedroom, where a wolf breaks into her room in a magnificent sequence. She wakes screaming.

This ending seems in sharp contrast to Carter's. Indeed, sexuality becomes, in this final moment of the film, a simple horror which it is neither in Carter's stories nor indeed in the rest of Jordan's film. Jordan himself seemed unhappy with the force of this final image and argued that the poem which the girl recites on the soundtrack undercuts that force. 'I didn't want the film to end with the girl under threat; it's a liberation in a way.'[18] However, Jordan himself seems to have taken a very bleak view of sexual relations at that period. His next film, *Mona Lisa* (1986), was in his own words about 'a man and a woman who may as well live on different planets, with no comprehension'. Bob Hoskins is a small-time villain who, having served a jail sentence, returns to a London he cannot recognize and falls in love with the prostitute Cathy Tyson, whom he escorts from job to job. A stylish and successful *noir* thriller, the film's focus is on a simple man adrift in a world he no longer understands; a world of mixed races and bought sex, where the simpler codes of an earlier age no longer apply.

At the centre of this incomprehensible world is the incomprehensibility of sexual difference. Women in this film are a) prostitutes and b) unfathomable. The happy ending involves Hoskins abandoning the enigmas posed by his 'black tart' as he walks off into the sunset of homosocial bliss with his chum Robbie Coltrane.

This third film marked another economic step up for both Jordan and Palace, but the next film, *High Spirits* (1988), was a step too far. Jordan still thinks that, if the film had been made on a low budget and in black and white, it could have been a vintage Ealing comedy. Given Jordan's striking ability to take on new genres, it would be foolish to discount his opinion completely, but it is difficult to understand how this tale of American tourists visiting a haunted castle in Ireland was ever going to be more than an excuse to film Hollywood stars against a number of stage-Irish settings. When the original leads, Sean Connery and Jeff Daniels, pulled out and as the American producers that Palace had found became more and more intrusive, the film descended into considerable acrimony. Jordan never saw the final version, which was critically mauled and performed poorly at the box office.

Before *High Spirits* was released, Jordan was in America working directly for Paramount shooting a David Mamet script, *We're No*

Angels (1989), with Robert De Niro, Sean Penn and Demi Moore. It is the only time Jordan has worked as a director for hire and it left him with no desire to repeat the experience. He remains proud of the finished film, although it performed as poorly as *High Spirits* at the box office. Despite these failures, there was no shortage of offers to direct in America. Directing is one of the most taxing of jobs. During a shoot the director has literally hundreds of people looking to him for decisions, from where Sean Penn will stand to questions of set design and costume. If, at any point, the cast and crew lose faith in the director's ability to make these decisions, chaos ensues. Whatever the box office returns of his last two films, Jordan had proved his ability to direct big-budget movies and could have spent the rest of his life lucratively directing for the studios.

The Miracle: A Fresh Start

But Jordan was now clear that he was only really happy directing his own work and he was also keen to get back to Ireland to see more of his children. What he did was effectively to make a fresh start and for this purpose he returned to his collection of short stories, *Night in Tunisia*. Some authorities describe *The Miracle* (1991) as an adaptation of the longest and title story in the collection *Night in Tunisia*,[19] but this is extremely misleading. Several of the stories are set in holiday resorts in the summer and Jordan's film draws on all of them to create an entirely new story.

It is as if he had turned back to material from adolescence now rewritten by a man whose first marriage has ended and whose second has not yet begun.

The Miracle is nothing less than the miracle of sexual desire: how is it possible to desire a woman when the first woman you have desired – the mother – must be renounced utterly. If it was fair to say of *Mona Lisa* that the question of sexual difference was abandoned as unanswerable, it is also fair to say that *The Miracle* confronts it head-on. Set in the seaside resort of Bray outside Dublin, the film focuses on a young man, Jimmy, who is unable to transform his friendship with a girl his own age into desire and who despises his alcoholic single parent of a father. A mysterious older woman appears in the resort and Jimmy falls in love with her. The woman is his mother, whmo Jimmy had believed dead.

Here the Oedipus complex is not an interpretative grid for the story but the substance of the narrative itself. In a piece of casting which truly beggars belief, Jordan cast his real lover, Beverley D'Angelo, as his imaginary mother. The trick, however, worked. The scenes between the boy and the mother are genuinely unsettling as we rub up against incest, the defining human taboo. In a moving final sequence, when the boy has renounced the mother and accepted his father's weakness, the miracle, assisted by an array of religious statues, occurs. Jimmy is rewarded with the love of the girl whose body can now be desired in its bloody difference. In its concern with a weak and drunken father, in its use of popular culture, in its easy movement between dream and reality, *The Miracle* uncannily foreshadows *The Butcher Boy*. It is also clearly Jordan's first mature work. Maturity is the ability to draw on one's whole range of experience and *The Miracle* effortlessly moves between the adolescent memories of a seaside resort in summer and a whole gamut of cultural forms, from the Hollywood Western through big band music to the poetry of Yeats. It is impossible not to think of Yeats's 'The Circus Animals' Desertion' (1939) as the film comes to its end and the miracle of desire is announced by the escape of the animals from the circus. It is the circus which has provided a sub-plot in which the girl can discover the animality missing from the golf courses where her father passes his life. In *Angel*, the theme of the film had been stated by one of the characters: 'men start out as angels and end up as brutes'. *The Miracle* suggests that there may be a way to render the brutal angelic. Yeats writes his poem as his life comes to an end and he sees all his great themes as circus animals who have now deserted him, leaving him nothing but their origin: 'the foul rag and bone shop of the heart'. In *The Miracle*, the circus animals announce not the end of a great creative surge but the beginning. Jordan, himself not a great self-praiser, calls it 'a lovely little movie'.

The Crying Game and Hollywood Success

The next film that Jordan set himself to make was originally called *A Soldier's Wife*. The theme – the relation between an IRA unit and the British soldier they hold hostage – had a long pedigree in Irish letters. It had been the subject matter of Brendan Behan's play *The Hostage* (1958), which itself drew inspiration from a Frank O'Connor short story, 'Guests of the Nation' (1931). Jordan wrote the first drafts after *Angel* and gave two twists to the tale. First, the soldier was black and the events that end in the hostage's death occupy only the first half of the screenplay. The second twist moves the action to London, where the IRA volunteer who befriended the hostage before his death seeks out the dead man's wife. Jordan wanted to write about the London that he had known as an immigrant worker in the early seventies, but the script got bogged down until Jordan added a further twist – he turned the dead soldier's wife into a transvestite.

The film did not get off to a good start. The financing was much the same as *The Miracle* – the major partners were Channel 4 and British Screen, the then British state subsidy arm for commercial cinema, and Palace. But the recession and Nik Powell's tremendous desire to produce movies had turned a successful distribution company into one heading for bankruptcy and the film, a much more ambitious production, was continually short of money.[20] On its release, some Irish critics claimed it dealt in IRA stereotypes and a British public whose reaction to Ireland throughout the modern chapter of The Troubles had been one of a studied lack of interest failed to turn up. However, on its release in the States, an inspired marketing campaign[21] and a world in which, to use Derek Jarman's words, 'everyone wants a touch of black cock'[22] combined to deliver a hit, huge sums of money and an Oscar.

It is appropriate that Jaye Davidson, who played the transvestite, Dil, was 'discovered' at the wrap party for Jarman's *Edward II*. One of that film's themes is the structural relationship between male homosexual desire and misogyny, and that structure is also central to Jordan's film.[23] The black soldier is lured to his death by a flaunting of female sexuality and the narrative takes its revenge when, at the end, this deadly sexuality is brutally extinguished. Jordan was to investigate this theme further in his next film, *Interview with the Vampire* (1994). One of the most enthusiastic viewers of *The Crying Game* had been David Geffen. Geffen had started in the post room at the William Morris Agency, but through the seventies and eighties he had become one of the most successful entrepreneurs in the music business, finally selling his own label for over half a billion dollars at the beginning of the nineties. Later in the decade he would be one of the trio (with Steven Spielberg and Jeffrey Katzenberg) who would set up a new studio called Dreamworks, but his first move into the film industry was a deal with Warner Brothers. *The Crying Game* had convinced Geffen that Jordan was the man to direct the film of a book for which he already held the rights, Anne Rice's best-selling *Interview with the Vampire* (1976). Jordan claims that he found the novel 'extraordinarily captivating', but it is easier to believe his more muted claim that he remains 'quite happy with the script'. In fact the transformation of a long rambling novel spanning two centuries into a tight narrative could be used as a master class in adaptation.

Orson Welles famously described a Hollywood studio as 'the biggest train set a boy ever had'. There is no doubt that much of the attraction of Geffen's project for Jordan was that it held out the promise of real access to the train set in a way that being a director for hire did not. The promise was honoured: from the casting of Tom Cruise and Brad Pitt through the burning down of a plantation on the banks of the Mississippi to a score which is composed with historically accurate instruments, Jordan had access to resources on a scale he had never before enjoyed. However, the film remains a genre exercise, and its most striking scenes are slow murders of beautiful and terrified young women in which the skill of the director makes us complicit with the pleasures of sadism.

4

FROM NOVEL TO FILM-SCRIPT
....

First Drafts

It was as Jordan was editing *Interview with the Vampire* that Patrick McCabe presented him with his second draft of *The Butcher Boy*. Jessica Scarlata voices a common critical opinion, both journalistic and academic, when she says that the ending of the film is 'one of its few departures from the plot of the novel.'[24]

In fact, there are a great number of changes from the novel, some of the most important of which date from McCabe's first draft of July 1993. At two of the crisis points in the novel, the moment before shitting on the Nugent's floor and the moment before he attacks Fr Tiddly for a second time, Francie imagines himself as Mrs Nugent's child in the most literal sense:

> Then I heard Philip Nugent's voice. But it was different now, all soft and calm. He said: You know what he's doing here don't you mother? He wants to be one of us. He wants his name to be Francis Nugent. That's what he's wanted all along! We know that – don't we mother?
>
> Mrs Nugent was standing over me. Yes, Philip she said. I know that. I've known it for a long time.
>
> Then slowly she unbuttoned her blouse and took out her breast.
>
> Then she said: This is for you Francis.
>
> She put her hand behind my head and firmly pressed my face forward. Philip was still at the bottom of the bed smiling. I cried out: *Ma! It's not true!* Mrs Nugent shook her head and said: *I'm sorry Francis it's too late for all that now. You*

should have thought of that when you made up your mind to come and live with us!

I thought I was going to choke on the fat lukewarm flesh.

No! (*The Butcher Boy*, p. 60)

In the novel there are two attacks on Fr Tiddly. The second, and more vicious, occurs when Francie, under pressure from Tiddly, has described the Nugents' house as his own and he imagines Mrs Nugent speaking to Ma Brady:

Do you know what he did? He asked me to be his mother. He said he'd give anything not to be a pig. That's what he did on you Mrs Brady. That's why he came to our house! Her breast was choking me again, lukewarm in my throat. (*The Butcher Boy*, p. 91)

Mrs Nugent's breast had disappeared from both scenes in McCabe's first draft. As well as these deletions there is one significant addition when, in a short scene at the Industrial School, Francie has a brief conversation with Our Lady in which Our Lady speaks. In the novel there is no suggestion that the Blessed Virgin actually appears to Francie; her reality is guaranteed by the naïvety of priests and bogmen. However, for the most part this first draft is an all-too-faithful rendition of the book, although alcohol, particularly through an additional scene in Dublin, is even more of a theme than in the novel.

Apart from other reservations, the problem with this first script was that it is far too long – the resulting film would have numbed bums for over three hours. McCabe's second effort, finished at the end of 1993, is much tighter. There is a great deal of compression – both Uncle Alo's arrival and Francie's return for his mother's funeral are staged in the Diamond in the centre of Clones, both emphasizing the town's reality and excising unnecessary secondary business. Also Joe's friendship becomes much more central. After his mother's suicide, Francie's solitary thought that 'As long as I walked the streets under them stars there'd be only one thing anyone could say about me and that was: I hope he's proud of himself now, the pig, after what he did on his poor mother' (p. 44) is now shared with Joe. When Francie is led in symbolic chains from the Nugent household, Joe is there to swear undying loyalty.

The Virgin Mary's speaking part is considerably expanded in a scene in which she consoles Francie about the goldfish that Philip gave to Joe. However, the breakdown of the friendship with Joe is lengthy and undramatic and McCabe, demonstrating the fertility of the world of *Carn*, invents a long and complicated subplot in which Leddy the pig slaughterer and Sergeant Sausage – both suitors in their youth of Francie's mother – keep a weather-eye on young Francie as pledges of their youthful ardour. This subplot flickers through the pages of the novel and there are traces of it in the finished film, particularly the very opening scene by Francie's hospital bed. However, when this subplot is moved into the foreground, it loses the novel's focus as we vacillate between Francie and his dead mother.

Jordan now decided to try a draft himself and, going back to the original book, with McCabe's two drafts in hand, he wrote a new and third draft in the astonishing period, vouched for by both Woolley and McCabe, of three days. Jordan's brilliance as a director has perhaps detracted attention from his career as an amazingly prolific writer. The most salient fact of this particular burst of creativity was not a third draft but the fact that Jordan felt himself possessed by Francie's voice and so decided, for the first time, that he would direct the film himself.

Michael Collins

The politics of the Hollywood studios demand their own anthropology. While the bottom line is determining, that bottom line is dependent above all on the cinema's biggest economic asset: stars. How far a studio can attract stars is crucial to the studio's economic performance and how far they can attract stars is dependent on many variables: money is one but reputation is another. *Interview with the Vampire* grossed over $100,000,000 in the US. The average for a Tom Cruise vehicle at that time was nearer $150,000,000, but Warners had been going through a lean time at the box office and to have a hit, the magic nine numbers, was significant for studio morale. Perhaps as important was the controversy the film had engendered over the casting of Cruise. Anne Rice had taken out a full-page advertisement in *Variety* to denounce the decision, then had taken out another one to congratulate the makers after seeing the film. You cannot buy aesthetic integrity, but any Los Angeles PR firm would tell you that such controversy was priceless. Casting action man Cruise as a faggy little leather boy in a blond wig had been daring on both sides. Audacity and skill, again on both sides, was rewarded. The studio was pleased and asked Jordan what he wanted to do next. The answer was the same one that he had given to anyone who asked for over ten years: *Michael Collins*. It might even be an advantage, added Jordan, that if they looked in their files they would find that they already owned the script.

In reviewing Jordan's career, one of its most admirable features is his refusal to be caught in development hell. If one project stalls, then he will do another; if he cannot make this thriller then he will do that comedy; if he cannot film a love story then he will shoot a horror film. A necessary condition of this ducking and diving is his relentless productivity as a writer. There are parallels – Balzac and his debtors, Dostoevsky and his gambling, Moorcock and his three-day visions of the future – but none of them were harnessed to the world of options and rewrites. Once *Angel* had made it to the big screen, the offers poured in. One was from David Puttnam, then basking in the success of *Chariots of Fire* (1981). One topic that Puttnam suggested – with a juicy studio fee attached – was Michael Collins. To this day, Jordan says that when Puttnam made this suggestion Jordan himself knew practically nothing about Collins. Jordan was raised in the purple of

Irish education and published, just before *Angel*, a very fine novel, *The Past* (1980), whose opening chapters are set in the original 'Troubles'. It is difficult to give any credit to the statement that he knew nothing about one of the few legendary figures of modern Irish history, a central figure in the events that Jordan had fictionalized in his novel. Even discounting the determined naïvety with which Jordan confronts the world, his ignorance of Collins can only make sense as a professional claim. Jordan took his degree in history at University College Dublin with great seriousness and the claim must simply mean that he had not acquainted himself with the primary sources.[25]

This he now did and wrote the first of an endless succession of scripts. Puttnam's deal was with Warners and, when he became head of Columbia Pictures shortly after, he could not take the script with him. Jordan now lacked a champion at the studio and had to deal with a string of executives, all with their own take on the subject. To make matters worse, Puttnam, in his new role at Columbia, commissioned a Collins project from Michael Cimino. No sooner had Cimino's project collapsed than Kevin Costner announced that he would bring the story of Ireland's anti-colonial struggle to the screen.

My own sense of Collins is perhaps affected by family history. My father, Myles MacCabe, was born in Cavan, which borders Monaghan, on 22 August 1922, the day on which Collins, now in uniform as the commander-in-chief of the Irish Free State army, was shot and killed by an IRA flying column. Michael was the name my grandparents had chosen for a son, but in the aftermath of Collins's death this was changed to the more Gaelic Myles. Perhaps not surprisingly, my father took a great interest in Collins, devouring all books on the subject. He could wax eloquent on Collins's skill as a master of terror and muse, as so many of his generation did, on the Ireland that might have resulted had he lived; in particular, whether the democratic structures could have survived a charismatic military leader. But he was much more fascinated by the period at the end of 1921, when Collins was in London at the end of the War of

Independence, and by the dramatic moments leading up to the signing of the Treaty, which gained independence for twenty-six counties of Ireland but was to leave six as part of the United Kingdom. It was the rejection of that treaty by de Valera and the IRA that Collins had formed and led that was to result in the Civil War in which Collins died. As a child, my imagination was particularly engaged by the final evening of those talks, when Collins, broken in two by the conflicting claims on his soul, decided to sign. Churchill, who was negotiating beside Lloyd George, wrote that he had never seen a man in the grip of such emotion. The details of the Treaty settled at 9.00 in the evening, the Irish contingent went back to their hotel before putting their signatures to the document. The argument continued right up until the last moment as they patrolled the deserted streets of London before finally, at 2.30 in the morning, walking into 10 Downing Street. As he signed, Collins remarked presciently that he was signing his own death warrant.

The image of those Irishmen walking the streets of my native city debating their country's future with their own lives in the balance had always been a powerful one for me. As a child, this had been filed under history but by 1973 it was current, as the Provisional IRA visited a bombing campaign on London and brought the Civil War which had started in Belfast and Derry in 1969 to what some called The Mainland. From 1969 the ancient debate between pro- and anti-Treaty, between Free Staters and the IRA, was ancient no more and Collins himself, the man of violence who had decided on a compromise peace, was a figure of immediate relevance. Indeed in the late 1980s, while Head of Production at the British Film Institute, I had commissioned the poet and critic Tom Paulin to write a film script on Collins to be directed by Thaddeus O'Sullivan. The brief I sketched out was simple: focus on the months in London, think even of setting the whole film on that final night.

That project never got out of development, so, when in April 1992 Jordan told me that he had written a script on Collins, I could hardly wait to read it. I had just seen an early screening of *The Crying Game*, which confirmed the promise of *The Miracle* – Jordan was now a major director. I have rarely started reading a script with more excitement. I have certainly never been so bitterly disappointed. Collins's time in London was not even mentioned – it was *Hamlet* without the Prince. Indeed what I seemed to be reading was a conventional epic, the nation taking form around a great hero. This particular genre had been trademarked early by Virgil and its most recent outings on British screens had been David Lean's *Lawrence of Arabia* (1962) and Richard Attenborough's *Gandhi* (1982). Jordan's script seemed to me untrue to the man and irrelevant to the country.

About the latter I could not have been more wrong. Jordan's diary of the production gives a vivid sense of bringing to life a long-buried national trauma and on its release in Ireland *Michael Collins* not only broke all box-office records but started a national debate about the past which broke the academic confines of revisionist and nationalist historians to offer Irish men and women fresh access to their own history. Jordan's originality was to tell Collins's story as an entirely heroic one. This involved avoiding the complexities of the London negotiations and thus managing to avoid the endless pro- and anti-Treaty debates which had been bogged down within well-worn ruts for over seven decades. Jordan would argue that he had written not an epic but a tragedy and that Collins's death avoids any unproblematic notion of a movie which tells a story of national liberation. But if Jordan's film diary is very aware of the complexities of history, his film is less so.

It is certainly open to criticism for its apparent endorsement of political violence, an endorsement which Jordan accentuates by shooting the central section of the film as a gangster movie, with whole sequences stolen[26] from Coppola's *Godfather* films. It also means that the end of the film, including the magnificent and moving sequence which sees Collins meet his death, is incomprehensible to any audience not already familiar with Ireland's politics.

The link between art and politics is difficult to establish. When one has abandoned the Romantic arrogance of legislating for the future and the Leninist arrogance of serving the people, the questions of cause and effect remain. Yeats famously wondered whether 'that play of mine sent out certain men the English shot'. Jordan has the more enviable task of pondering the role that *Michael Collins* played in the referendum on the peace process, when the vast majority of Irish people voted to renounce an absolute claim of sovereignty over the six counties of the North. It would be ludicrous to claim that this film was a determining element in that decision, but it would be equally ludicrous to say that it was not a significant element in the debates that led up to it. It might be said that the film provided a cultural legitimation for the twenty-six county state of 1922.[27]

Luke Gibbons records some baffled American fan exiting a multiplex saying that the Collins figure was 'awesome' but that the 'gay Nazi dude sucked'.[28] The 'gay Nazi dude' refers to Alan Rickman's awesome performance as Eamon de Valera, the figure who dominated Irish politics for the first forty years of independence. Clearly the performance depends in large measure on knowledge of the original. Jordan had made an historical epic for his people, but, by that very token, the film bombed at the American box office, barely crawling past the $10m mark.

Warners, however, were still pleased. They had foreseen a poor performance at the American box office and had consequently set the price very low indeed – $25,000,000 for an historical epic which involved, amongst other things, destroying the centre of Dublin twice. So low was the budget that Jordan and Woolley had to throw their fees into the pot. But the money went a long way. The combination of production skills honed in the independent sector and a tremendous desire to get the film made delivered a genuine Irish epic.

Warners were still very pleased with Jordan. *Michael Collins* had garnered huge critical plaudits. It won not only Best Film at the

Venice Film Festival but also Best Actor for Liam Neeson's Collins. Hollywood gossip was more than impressed that a film on such a huge scale could have been produced on such a relatively modest budget and if the box office was poor the studio could take consolation from the regular television earnings that a film starring both Liam Neeson and Julia Roberts could expect into the indefinite future. Jordan and Woolley got their fees and, once again, Jordan was asked what he wanted to do next. A very small Irish film that you would not be interested in, he protested. The studio insisted, and very shortly *The Butcher Boy* was a greenlit production in an American studio.

5

A HOLLYWOOD PRODUCTION IN CLONES

The Language of Monaghan

It is worth pausing for a moment to reflect on what an extraordinary economic moment this was. A Hollywood studio was willing to underwrite a small Irish film to the tune of about $12,000,000. What this money bought was time – a relatively relaxed eleven-week schedule with five-day weeks – and space – the ability to dress sets so that the camera could shoot wide. It also ensured the money for the new digital effects, so crucial to the film's aesthetic. At the same time, the budget was so low that the studio would hardly bother with it. Once a film has passed out of the hands of the 'creatives' – the part of the studio that makes investment – it passes into the hands of 'physical production' – the industrial factory which concerns itself with matching schedule to budget. In physical production, the questions of juggling genre and story, star and role, against projected box-office returns are irrelevant. The questions in physical production are much more basic. Is the production keeping to its schedule? Do the daily rushes demonstrate technical competence? Is the director shooting enough angles on the scene to give the editor the 'cover' he or she needs? Only if the answers to these very practical questions are negative will the physical production executives alert the creatives that they must intervene. Once the studio had greenlit a script in which a boy kills his mother by running away from home, seems unbothered by his abuse at the hands of the clergy and finally performs a miraculous sacrifice by killing and gutting a harmless and unremarkable woman, its only way of protecting its investment is to let the director have his way, because the investment is entirely in the director and the bizarre tale he wishes to tell. Indeed, with such a small budget the additional overheads of having Los Angeles executives ride herd in County Monaghan was a strong disincentive to interfere with this particular example of Irish lunacy.

It is still surprising that Jordan was allowed to make the film in McCabe's language. Hollywood, ever since the Hays Code, has demanded a standard American English for its films. Any strong local accent is anathema. However, for both McCabe and Jordan, the language was crucial. This was to be a film shot in the accents of Monaghan and all the actors who were not native speakers went to considerable trouble to master this tongue, which is neither Dublin drawl nor Belfast rasp. Stephen Rea, for example, was to spend two days with McCabe making sure he could get the inflections right and indeed Benny Brady and Francie's voice-over in the film sound very similar to Patrick McCabe.

Perhaps unwisely, the first and only time the studio voiced its reservations in a memo, it chose to focus on the number of swearwords rather than the accent in which they were pronounced. McCabe's neat schoolmasterly memo in reply came with the following letterhead:

My fucking fax no
Cunting Bastarding tel no
THE EFFING BLINDING FILES
By Francis Brady
2, Bastard Lane
Hoortown
Co. Bollocks

It was followed by five pages in which McCabe's demotic inventiveness offered ever more unacceptable alternatives to the lines which had offended sensibilities. Wisely, the studio withdrew: Jordan had as free a hand as the economics of filmmaking allow.

Dublin gossip reduces the complicated development of the script to an exasperated Jordan taking over from a prolix McCabe and introducing order into chaos. In fact, Jordan's third draft, written in August 1994 while editing *Interview with the Vampire*, is close to McCabe's second. Jordan drops McCabe's new material but retains most of McCabe's adaptations. McCabe says that Jordan was generous to give him an equal credit for the final script, but an examination of the extant drafts suggests that Jordan was fair as well as generous. In any case, throughout the writing process Jordan relied on McCabe for advice and comments, knowing that McCabe's knowledge of Clones dialogue was always going to be vastly superior to his own. Whatever gossip says, this was a genuine collaboration.

Violence

Two years and *Michael Collins* were to intervene before Jordan turned again to Francie Brady to write a fourth script, and now he did make a fundamental change which would differentiate the film from the novel. It was a change, however, which he made as a director rather than a writer. In the book Francie moves from schoolboy to adolescent and, if the film was to follow faithfully this physical and psychological curve, then two actors would be needed. As he sat down to the fourth script, Jordan decided that the part could only be played by one actor and in the script dated March 1996 Francie remains a child, as he does in the film, from beginning to end. In the last quarter of the book, when he has been officially released from the mental hospital, Francie terrifies everyone who meets him. In a state of hypermania and suffering from paranoid delusions, Francie revels in his new-found physical power to humiliate and hurt. Fuelled by alcohol, he wanders through the last pages of the book in a ridiculously oversized and filthy jacket inspiring fear wherever he goes. He terrorizes Mrs Connolly, one of the women who jests with him in the shop and who has cleaned his house for his return to the town from the mental hospital. When he gets to Bundoran he is a walking incitement to argument and, when he returns to the town after being thrown out of Joe's school, he makes Mrs Nugent beg for her life and beats her up before he shoots her.

As readers, we barely register these details. We are overwhelmed by the crushing burden of rejection that Francie is accumulating and we continue to be exhilarated by Francie's torrent of words. As viewers, the details of Francie's actions would be central. McCabe's drafts had downplayed this violence and Jordan eliminates it all, except for the actual murder of Mrs Nugent.

Although there would be a fifth draft and many further revisions during shooting and editing, particularly to the voice-over, the script of the film we know was fundamentally in place. Bazin found the key to adaptation to be the development of specific cinematic material which extended the original work. Jordan's decision to keep Francie as a boy was part and parcel of eliminating much of the extreme violence which dominates the end of the book. However, the movie does not simply renounce this violence. Film can deliver violence at a speed and with a realism which is beyond the powers of prose. From the moment thirty minutes into *Mona Lisa* that Bob Hoskins brutally attacks a pimp and changes the whole tone of that film, Jordan had demonstrated that he is a master of screen violence. Francie erupts three times in the film: when he attacks Buttsy with a stone, when he stabs Fr Tiddly with a paper knife and when he kills Mrs Nugent with his humane killer. On each occasion the swiftness and ferocity of the attack is shocking.

These moments show Jordan using the resources of cinema to bring the book to life on the screen. As important, however, is the way the film, doing what no book could do, weaves violence into both image and audience through the metaphor of the mushroom cloud of the atomic bomb. By using this most powerful of icons, Jordan links the violence in Francie's life to the violence in the species.

The dropping of the atomic bombs on Nagasaki and Hiroshima announced that man's death drive could conceivably annihilate human civilization. The threat of atomic death, in the form of the Cuban missile crisis, is a constant motif of the novel – 'It will be a bitter day for this town if the world comes to an end' – but Jordan

Plate 2.   Francie and Joe wander through the town after it has been destroyed by an atomic bomb

knits the mushroom cloud into the very fabric of the film. When Francie is conducting his School for Pigs in the Nugent house, the novel has him watching *Voyage to the Bottom of the Sea* on the television, but the film shows footage from an imaginary atomic attack on the small screen. Indeed, the mushroom cloud has already appeared in a scene which is completely reworked from the novel. As Da Brady beats Francie for stealing Philip Nugent's comics and Ma Brady reaches for Dr Roche's useless tablets, an atomic bomb erupts on the screen and a voice-over asks whether mankind will be able to control the dream that he has just realized. These black-and-white images explode in full colour in the film's single most memorable image as Francie experiences total psychotic collapse when his demented attempts to deny his father's death are overwhelmed by reality. Lacan teaches us that what has been rejected in the symbolic returns in the real and there can be few more striking demonstrations of this dictum than the sequence in Jordan's film which juxtaposes the moment when Francie is forced to accept that his father is dead with his fantasy of an atomic explosion in the lake where he and Joe have played as Red Indians. Francie is completely unable to symbolize his father's death and the result is the hallucination of a death which affects the whole town.

The film's use of television to develop and emphasize the violence of atomic death is also a development and emphasis of television itself. On 31 December 1961 Eamon de Valera, now President after decades as Prime Minister, addressed the nation. The occasion was the introduction of a national television service and the President was in sombre mood.

As Martin McLoone notes, he told his audience that television was 'Like atomic energy, it can be used for incalculable good but it can also do irreparable harm.'[29] De Valera must have suspected that the advent of television spelled the end of the cultural isolation that his policies had promoted for over four decades. From the censorship of books and films to the neutrality that kept it out of World War II, Ireland under de Valera had deliberately isolated itself from Yeats's 'filthy modern tide'. *The Butcher Boy* confirms de Valera's fears that television offered a completely different access to the world than that afforded by the Catholic Church with its Eucharistic Congresses and its missions to the Balubas.

Dead Mothers

A further consequence of the decision to keep Francie as a child is that it becomes implausible that he be released from the mental hospital as he is in the novel. Jordan's solution is an escape which not only cuts out the whole narrative sequence in which Francie degenerates into disturbed violence, but also provides a symbolic link between the beginning and the end of the film. Francie's escape from the mental hospital is through a window and this escape 'rhymes' back to Francie's first escape, when he fled his parents' home after Alo's party. Rhyme in poetry produces equivalences through form and in the film it emphasizes the equivalence between Ma Brady and Mrs Nugent: both Francie's escapes culminate with the death of a mother.[30]

The way in which stories articulate the psychic and the social – providing in characters and their transformations access both to internal emotions and external reality – is what makes narrative so fundamental to our human condition. As we trace the story of Francie Brady from 'Baby Pig' to the published novel to Jordan's film, the determining change, the deepest emotional level of which McCabe speaks, is a focus on the death of the mother. It is a focus the film sharpens. In 'Baby Pig', as in the source text, *He Lies in Armagh Jail*, one friend, Francie, kills another, Joe. In 'Baby Pig' the death comes in the slaughterhouse as Joe tries to persuade Francie to come with him to America for a holiday. But Francie is too conscious of the class divisions that now prevent any desired reunion: 'Then he smoothed back his hair that way. As long as I'd known him before he went away to the boarding school he had never touched his hair like that' ('Baby Pig', p. 94). Francie's resentment provokes Joe to fury: 'Stay here then!' he said 'Stay with the pigs if that's where you belong' ('Baby Pig', p. 96).

Francie's response is to butcher him.

In the novel Francie is caught between two impossible mothers: his own is so weak that she could not even nourish him in her womb, and Mrs Nugent is so overpowering that if he thinks of her as his mother he finds himself choking. Throughout the book he is looking for a father whose desire will magically restore his own mother to strength and end the threat of suffocation posed by Mrs Nugent. The end of the book sees the total collapse of these hopes. The family romance of Bundoran, the promise that he is the result of a genuine moment of desire, a moment that will cancel all the rows and drunkenness, proves only that his father is a pig:

'No better than a pig, the way he disgraced himself here. Any man who'd insult a priest the way he did. Poor Fr

> McGivney who wouldn't hurt a fly . . . God knows he works hard enough in the orphanage in Belfast without having to endure abuse the like of what that man gave him.' (*The Butcher Boy*, p. 181)[31]

The grammatical construction invites us to ask what abuse and what man? Indeed there is every reason to think that it is the abuse that Benny Brady has suffered in the orphanage that ruins the honeymoon in Bundoran and renders Francie's image of masculinity hopelessly broken. When his symbolic universe collapses, Francie's only choice is to murder Mrs Nugent, for that is his only means of access to the symbolic world – his only chance of claiming an identity in a town which can find no place for him. But in murdering Mrs Nugent Francie is murdering the image of the Church that has humiliated and disgraced the Bradys. As Francis Brady sticks his hands into Mrs Nugent's stomach and writes PIGS all over the walls of the upstairs room, he comes as close as he ever does to Patrick McCabe writing the novel that we are reading.

Pat McCabe and Jim Joyce

The problem of weak fathers and overpowering mothers is written deep into Ireland's history and provides the theme of Ireland's greatest writer, James Joyce. It is possible to read *The Butcher Boy* as an updated version of *A Portrait of the Artist as a Young Man* (1916) and parallel after parallel can be drawn – most powerfully at Uncle Alo's party, where the famous Christmas dinner scene of *A Portrait* gets replayed. The end, however, is significantly different, with Stephen leaving Ireland to search for the father that he cannot find at home. In Joyce's own life the choice of exile is inevitable once he decides to link his own life to the chambermaid Nora Barnacle. He knows that this relationship which crosses class boundaries will not be tolerated in Ireland and what he will write is bound to offend the 'archons of Sinn Féin'. For Joyce, all that awaits him in a state founded on the prejudices of Irish nationalism is the noggin of hemlock that the archons of Athens prepared for Socrates. The bitter truth of this exile is that Joyce will have no Irish child. This truth is one of the key motifs of *Ulysses*.

At the end of the 'Circe' sequence in *Ulysses*, Bloom's son, dead almost as soon as he was born, appears as the eleven-year-old child he would have been. He is dressed in an Eton suit with a lambkin peeping out of his pocket, a costume which incarnates the limited dream of the Gaelic revival merging a nice English middle-class boy with a fantasy Irish peasant, a Philip Nugent before his time.

Joyce has to go outside Ireland and England to find the symbolic support which will enable him to find a place in the world, but McCabe has no such need, for he finds it in the language which so thrills us as we read the book. At the end of *Portrait*, in a scene which is perhaps the most famous and quoted of all Joyce's work, Stephen has a discussion about language with the Dean of his university, who is English. Joyce uses the word 'tundish', meaning funnel – a word from Elizabethan English which is still current in Irish English but archaic in British English. Stephen, throughout the conversation, knows that his grasp of the language is superior to his Dean's, but he reflects that it is 'his [language] before it is mine' and that his own 'soul frets in the shadow of his language'. There can be no doubt that for McCabe Francie's language is the language of his own soul and, like Francie, he has no doubt of its superiority to British English, at least in part because of the achievement of Joyce as the greatest master of English that the literary tradition has produced. Joyce, however, cannot find a language for his soul in his own country. Ireland outside Dublin, the Ireland of Davin, the peasant student, is a mystery. Dublin itself is a centre of paralysis, caught in the most sterile of repetitions. The closest character to Francie Brady in *Ulysses* is the nameless narrator of Bloom's encounter with the Citizen in Barney Kiernan's pub. However, the energy and inventiveness of the Nameless One's monologue has nothing of the innocence and optimism of Francie's narration. It is impossible to identify with the bitter cynicism and sterile vision of Dublin's inhabitants in *Ulysses*.

Francie Brady finds in the language of Clones a resource and identification which is not available to Stephen Dedalus in Dublin.

But, if region differentiates McCabe from Joyce, so does class. Joyce was well aware of the vitality of Anglo-Saxon popular culture, but the narrator of 'An Encounter' in *Dubliners* makes clear the class barrier which separates him from it:

> Everyone's heart palpitated as Leo Dillon handed up the paper and everyone assumed an innocent face. Father Butler turned over the pages, frowning.
>
> –What is this rubbish? he said. *The Apache Chief*! Is this what you read instead of studying your Roman History? Let me not find any more of this wretched stuff in this college.
>
> The man who wrote it, I suppose, was some wretched fellow who writes these things for a drink. I'm surprised at boys like you, educated, reading such stuff! I could understand it if you were . . . National School boys. Now, Dillon, I advise you strongly, get at your work or . . .
>
> This rebuke during the sober hours of school paled much of the glory of the Wild West for me, and the confused puffy face of Leo Dillon awakened one of my consciences. But when the restraining influence of the school was at a distance I began to hunger again for wild sensations, for the escape which these chronicles of disorder alone seemed to offer me. The mimic warfare of the evening became at last as wearisome to me as the routine of school in the morning because I wanted real adventures to happen to myself. But real adventures, I reflected, do not happen to people who remain at home: they must be sought abroad.[32]

McCabe is remarkable in that he is determined to find these adventures at home and in his own language. This is what makes

McCabe's book so remarkable, this is why it was greeted as a radical step forward by many of Ireland's writers, including Jordan. The importance of the novel for Irish culture is a major reason why Jordan was able to assemble such an extraordinary cast for the film. Certainly Stephen Rea's acceptance of the relatively small part of Da Brady was because he realized how determined Jordan was to recognize the importance of what McCabe had done for the Irish novel and to produce a film with its energy and optimism, not a drab little film about social victims.

The Cast

Stephen Rea has been Jordan's actor of choice since *Angel*; like John Wayne for Ford, like Jean-Pierre Léaud for Truffaut, it is Rea who has been Jordan's privileged interlocutor. Jordan needed an actor of Rea's status for the role of Da Brady, because, like so many of the characters, Da Brady is very close to the stereotype of the drunken Irish father. Stereotypes, of course, find much of their force from the reality they figure, but to play Da Brady as simply an Irish drunk rather than a specific individual in the grip of a deadly addiction would be to collapse the figure of the novel into caricature. This is not just a problem of one character – it is a risk which runs through the entire script. Indeed, maintaining the balance between stereotype and individual was one of Jordan's major tasks as a director. It was all too easy for McCabe's characters to collapse into stage-Irish figures and Jordan often had to re-shoot – and on more than one occasion recast – when scenes degenerated as actors relapsed into stock characters. One crucial element which saved the film from this fate was the use of Stephen Rea to provide an adult voice for Francie which constantly works in dialogue with the image to resist all such easy blandishments.

If there were actors who fell by the wayside, the ones that remain are magnificent. Fiona Shaw as Mrs Nugent, Brendan Gleeson as Fr Bubbles, Aisling O'Sullivan as Ma Brady, Tom Hickey as the

Plate 3. Ma Brady (Aisling O'Sullivan)

Gardener – one could write a whole book simply reflecting on these performances and the way they play against both the stereotypes of the characters and the expectations that these actors, all familiar faces in Ireland, bring to their roles. To take one example, it was a stroke of genius to cast Milo O'Shea as the abusive Fr Tiddly. O'Shea is among the most famous of Irish actors, with a distinguished career at the Abbey Theatre as well as success in American film and television. His greatest role, however, has been as Leopold Bloom in Joseph Strick's *Ulysses* (1967) and, for anyone who has seen the film, it is almost impossible to dissociate his face from that Irish Everyman.

One of the features of Francie's narrative is that there are few villains in his story. As we read, it is Francie's appetite for life which dominates the action, but on the screen that appetite risks being swamped by the hideous fact of abuse. It is Milo O'Shea's familiar and reassuring face which renders the first scenes tolerable and it is his astonishing performance, in which so familiar and so friendly a face suddenly hardens into the rictus of exploitation, that makes the scene as powerful in the film as it is in the novel.

There would, however, be no film whatsoever without the central performance of Eamonn Owens as Francie. Jordan and his casting director, Susie Figgis, a constant collaborator since *The Company of Wolves*, spent weeks seeing thousands of children before finding, in a school not far from Clones, both Eamonn Owens and Alan Boyle (who played Joe). There can be no doubt about the superb performance that Jordan elicited and Rea says that he lived and breathed the part with the young boy. Of course this was not the first time that Jordan had cast a non-actor in a crucial role. In *The Crying Game* Jaye Davidson was completely untried and turned in a performance which received an Oscar nomination. Jordan's method of directing, which is to remind actors where they are in the story, seems particularly effective with novices.

Jordan says that he hesitated for some time as to who to cast in the lead, but it is difficult to believe the choice was very hard, for amongst all his other qualities Eamonn Owens looks just like a pig – not the long-snouted ones you find in the farmyard but their cartoon representation, which Disney has made so familiar, with scrunched-up broad faces. Indeed the film is best understood as a live-action cartoon. It is what the credits sequence tells us and it fits perfectly the world of comics and television shows which dominates Francie's thinking. Cartoon might seem like a derogatory term, but *The Butcher Boy* was shot in the 1990s when *The Simpsons* could reasonably claim to be the most acute and realistic example of popular art.

Mother Ireland

The end of the novel finds Francie Brady finally free of the social anxiety which propels him through much of his trajectory. In killing Mrs Nugent he identifies himself as a pig and accepts his expulsion from the middle-class world into the universe of the bogmen which he has spent so much of his life attempting to disavow. No one will let him down again, no one can hold out the promise of an illusory social order; he has found his real place. It is this symbolic identification which enables him at the end of the book to set out with a bogman, the sky orange overhead and tears streaming down his face. It would be tempting to say that Jordan provides a happy ending to replace McCabe's sad one, but it would be more accurate to say that, as with 'the wolf's tender paws', he had to come up with a cinematic equivalent of an unrepresentable ecstasy. In fact the film is able to outdo the book, because the decision to so clearly split the narration and the character means that the voice-over guarantees Francie's place in the world. The end of the novel is the start of the

Plate 4. The Butcher Boy

Plate 5. In the slaughter house

Plate 6. Francie's psychotic world reappears

film. This allows both a much more precise identification of Mrs Nugent's femininity and the possibility of a maternal function that is neither inadequate nor overpowering.

Sandy Powell, after a brilliant studentship in the school of Jarman in the late eighties, had been a regular as costume designer with Jordan since *The Miracle*. It was her idea to dress Mrs Nugent in violent greens, aligning her at one and the same time with the Wicked Witch of *The Wizard of Oz* (1939) and the Mother Ireland of dismal history. The result is that, when Francie butchers her, it is not simply Mrs Nooge who is getting the chop but the whole representation of Ireland that the middle classes had arrogated to themselves since the Gaelic revival – the whole tawdry story of Dark Rosaleen and Cathleen ní Houlihan.

Like A Virgin

It is the refusal of these representations which allows a new figure to appear. On 1 November 1950 Pope Pius XII addressed, from the balcony of St Peter's, an audience of more than a million faithful with an infallible statement. Eighty years earlier the first Vatican Council had pronounced the doctrine of Papal infallibility: that the Pope could not be mistaken when he pronounced *ex cathedra* any statement of faith or doctrine. In fact since 1870 no Pope had so pronounced and fifty-five years later Pius XII's 1950 address is still the only occasion on which a Pope has spoken infallibly. His statement had been a long time coming. For a hundred years senior cardinals and organizations of the faithful had been petitioning Rome to recognize what had been an article of faith in the West for over a thousand years, although it had no sanction whatsoever in the New Testament and had not arisen as a popular belief until centuries after the death of Christ. Five years after Hiroshima, in the year of Francie Brady's and Neil Jordan's birth, the Catholic Church might have felt that it was important to confirm a maternal figure that would offer the promise of eternal life against this most brutal of earthly deaths. Pius

XII announced that it was now an official doctrine of the Catholic Church that Mary, the Mother of God, did not die but was assumed directly into Heaven. The link between Mary's immortality and the death of the world was emphasized by the service prescribed for the celebration of this new holiday of obligation, which makes frequent reference to the Book of Revelations.[33]

The figure of Mary, combining motherhood and chastity, exalting women in so far as they avoid the arrows of desire, is a central feature of post-Protestant Catholicism and a dominant element of Irish Catholicism. In both novel and film the Saviour is barely glimpsed – it is his Mother who is omnipresent. It was in Fatima in 1917 that Mary appeared to three Portuguese children to warn against the Russian revolution and make prophesies regarding war in our era. The film makes specific reference to Fatima, but the appearance of the Virgin to peasant children prophesying and consoling against the terrors of war has been a significant feature of Catholicism in the last century. It is this figure of the desexualized mother, whose ability to avoid the corruption of the flesh in sex is what guarantees her against the corruption of the flesh in death, that Francie mocks with the murder of Mrs Nugent as the town waits for the Mother of God to appear.

Francie's efforts in the novel are rewarded in the film with a maternal figure who promises life without denying death. The single most striking difference between novel and film is the role that Sinead O'Connor embodies and which combines the traditional Irish iconography of the Mother of God and the Irish colleen. Jordan claims that the most important reason he cast O'Connor was her striking resemblance to the face of Mary in the statues that decorate all the churches of Ireland. There is no reason to doubt that this was a necessary condition of her casting, but O'Connor brought to her role a history and an image which made her both perfect and controversial. She had been expelled from school in her youth and, like Francie Brady, had been sent to reform school.

Although the nuns had given her a guitar, she had witnessed scenes of great misery, including a baby being forcibly taken from one of her friends. Her career had been outspoken and controversial, both in her fight for women's and children's rights and as a determined opponent of the Church. Her most Warholian moment had come on an edition of Saturday Night Live when she ended her set by tearing up a photo of John Paul II and shouting 'Fight the real enemy'.

Jordan had long admired her extraordinary voice and had used her version of the traditional song 'She Moved Through the Fair' on the soundtrack of the final fatal moments of *Michael Collins*, one of the many moments where Jordan achieves in the filmic codes a reconciliation between those who feel residual support for the IRA and the Free Staters. Casting Sinead O'Connor as the image of Irish womanhood in *The Butcher Boy* was a stroke of genius, for it is impossible to figure her in the position of willing servitude which had crippled Francie's mother nor in the position of willed rectitude which constitutes Mrs Nugent as more of a real bully in the film.

Perhaps most important of all, Sinead O'Connor embodied an attitude to sexuality and religion which spelt death to the masculine theocracy which had held sway over Ireland since the middle of the nineteenth century and which had used its grip on the institutions of the independent state to abuse generations of children. Jordan first met O'Connor when he sidled up to her at an awards ceremony and asked her, as his opening line, whether some particularly scurrilous piece of gossip involving blow jobs was accurate. They survived this rather abrupt introduction and became friends in London in the late eighties, when they lived close to one another. O'Connor had been born on the 8th of December, the Feast of the Immaculate Conception, and thus had a particular attachment to the figure that she calls the 'BVM' (Blessed Virgin Mary). When Jordan offered her the part, she had no hesitation at all about embodying the mother of God. From O'Connor's perspective, the BVM takes her place along with Barbie and a host of others as a general icon of femininity.

Plate 7. The Blessed Virgin appears to Francie

One of the most striking features of O'Connor's performance is its combination of the maternal and the erotic. This striking double performance repudiates traditions stretching back two millennia to Paul's founding of the early Church, traditions which had become the very definition of Irish Catholicism. For O'Connor herself, the thing was simple. To Francie she spoke as she would to her own son, then only a little younger than Eamonn Owens; but she had also summoned her boyfriend to the set in the hope that they could engage in a passionate tryst while she was still robed as the Blessed Virgin. Devout Catholics and adepts of courtly love may be relieved to know that this particular sacrilege proved a step too far, but the prospect obviously lent something to O'Connor's unforgettable performance.

An Impure Ireland

Many critics talk as if this erotic vision of the Blessed Virgin is Francie's fantasy, but she often appears in the frame independently of his point of view. In the logic of the film she is as real as any of the other characters, holding out a hope that has been earned by Francie's commitment to language and writing. Luke Gibbons, one of the most subtle and learned of Irish critics, has suggested to me that her appearance is a reference to the aisling tradition of Irish poetry, when in the dark days of the eighteenth century Irish poets would evoke a skywoman who promised deliverance to an Ireland figured under a variety of female names. Both Jordan and McCabe fiercely deny any such intention – indeed, McCabe all but denies knowledge of the genre. However, in such matters declarations of conscious intention are not determining. Cultural forms repeat and transform in a logic that can often bypass the conscious mind. But Gibbons' reading is against the grain of the entire text, in which Irish and the Gaelic traditions are never mentioned except in Mrs Nugent's name. Grace Nugent is the heroine of Maria Edgeworth's 1812 novel *The Absentee*, where she functions as the representative of the Irish and Gaelic traditions and is the subject of a famous popular tune and Gaelic poem, 'Gracey Nugent', which praises her long life.[34] This is hardly Francie's attitude. Yeats famously remarked that Romantic Ireland was dead and gone and in his remark gave it fresh life. Baby Pig's reply is that it is buried with Ma in the manure heap down by the river.

The brilliance of both novel and film is that they construct representations of Ireland which are as true to the mixture of American and English popular culture as they are to Francie's speech and his town. The extraordinary feat of the film is to find a style, a form and a design which, while representing all the key features of Francie's life, manages to convince us that in the unutterable pain of living there is an utterable joy in existence. Since the 1890s a persuasive and compelling ideology has appealed to the purity of the Irish mind and body. *The Butcher Boy* has no time for purity as it stages nuclear explosions in the most beautiful of Irish scenery and produces a kitsch Virgin Mary to bless the world. The beauty of *The Butcher Boy* is that it combines the most realistic representation of Irish smalltown life with the most realized of fantasies, the everyday dialogue of Clones with the soundtrack of popular music.

At its centre is an unspeakable act of violence as Francie Brady dispatches Mrs Nugent with his humane killer. In both the original murder case and in the ur-novel, 'Baby Pig', the violence erupts out of the class differentiation of post-emancipation Ireland, but in *The Butcher Boy* that violence is focused on the figure of nationalist mother, who is the site of this violence's symbolic reproduction. Even when in 1829 they had been made second-class citizens of the United Kingdom, Irish Catholics were more than aware that their island had no genuine political representation. Fathers were condemned to failure by the imaginary version of full citizenship that they could never attain. It could be argued psychoanalytically that the colonial subject is offered, by the evident failure of the father, a better chance to avoid that involuntary servitude that is imperial masculinity. The bitter facts of Irish history make clear that any such chance has been systematically blocked by over-compensatory mothers producing murderous mummy's boys, killing and dying to occupy the psychic space of imperial masculinity. In slaughtering Mrs Nugent, Francie is breaking with this cycle, opening up an ecstatic new reality.

Irish Studies and the Post-colonial

This Utopian reality has not been much investigated by the new field of Irish Studies. In its formidable learning and acute textual readings, Irish Studies can make English Studies look like an unfortunate poor relation. On the downside, Irish Studies often sounds like the Gaelic Athletics Association at prayer.[35] As debilitating for an analysis of contemporary Irish culture has been the almost total embrace of the post-colonial model of cultural and political analysis developed in India in the 1980s.

The analysis developed by Bengali scholars around the journal *Subaltern Studies* understood nationalism as essentially a product of the colonial state. Nationalism embodies the most fundamental of colonial subjugations: the necessity to respond to the colonial master on his own terms, to produce a political movement that will appropriate the state. The corresponding ideological necessity is to produce citizen subjects who are both different and the same. They are the same in that they conform to the imperial model of subjectivity, but different in that the content of that subjectivity is different, be it Irish or Indian. For this is the difference that justifies the political struggle.

What is lost along the way is everything that constituted different subjectivities and social relations. The general poverty, both political and cultural, of post-colonial states in the aftermath of independence – of which Ireland is merely one notorious example – is the inevitable result of nationalist struggles that have appropriated models of politics and culture wholesale from their oppressors.

The problem with this analysis, which in any case made much more sense in the specific Indian context in which it was elaborated, is that the post-colonial intellectual can do nothing except await the excluded differences re-emerging. No real action, or even thought, is possible because any such efforts will simply reappropriate those excluded differences for bourgeois reason and national state. The result is an endless critique of the present, which forever fails to provide the full political picture. For, if the *Subaltern Studies* analysis rejected the whole strategy of national liberation elaborated by the Third International, they did not repudiate the Leninist analysis which awarded priority to politics over every instance of economic and cultural life. This is why one reads so many dreary articles and books upbraiding this novel or that film for failing to provide the correct political analysis.

That very notion of a correct political analysis in fact depends on Lenin's particular conception of the party, where the scientific analysis of the class struggle is developed within that class struggle itself. If the subalternists rejected the industrial proletariat as the guarantee of correctness, they did not question the possibility of correctness itself. Needless to say, there are few post-colonial academics, unlike the Bengali subalternists, who could now rehearse Lenin's manic logic, but it is that logic which still animates post-colonial discourse's claim to the international solidarity and community once embodied in the Third International.

The Third International, of course, was itself the product of the failure of the Second International. The Second International brought together socialist parties of Europe in a determination to avoid the next war that competition for resources would visit on Europe. For more than twenty years before 1914, those socialist parties of Europe, confident in their growing trade union power and in the inevitable collapse of capitalism, had only one fear: that in their desperate desire to cling to their property, the owning classes would unleash imperialist war. For twenty years the Second International passed resolution after resolution which made the opposition to any future war the political priority for all socialists. When the war came it was not simply, as Lenin had foreseen, that the socialist parties were unable to stop it. Outside a few courageous individuals, there was not even token resistance. What Lenin had absolutely not foreseen was that the socialist parties of Europe would respond, without hesitation and ignoring all their own history, when the cry went up that Throne and Altar were in danger.

This moment was, of course, the birth of the modern Irish state, as Connolly, despairing of his fellow European socialists, sent word to Pearse and thus began the process which was to see the armed volunteers of the Irish Republican Brotherhood join forces with the armed militants of the Irish Citizen Army. It was this union that cried havoc and let loose the dogs of war on the streets of Dublin in Easter 1916. It is in this conjunction of nation and violence that we continue to amble like sheep to shambles or like pigs to Leddy's slaughterhouse.

Fraternity
The Butcher Boy takes us to the roots of nation and violence in the extraordinarily specific world not just of Ireland or of Monaghan but

of Clones. However, Francie Brady speaks not just of his town or Monaghan or the Irish but of the human condition. It is probable that all sons in their dependent being fantasize a father in control of his own existence. But this fantasy is fundamentally psychotic, and is one of the deepest roots of violence. The failure of the father is to be embraced rather than rejected. Those like Mrs Nugent who would reject it are those who will continue the cycle of violence. This is the mortal danger of class society.

In the more than two centuries since the French Revolution, we have heard much of both liberty and equality, but in psychological terms it is fraternity which is the crucial term in breaking with despotism, in finding a way to experience being in which dependency and autonomy co-exist. Ireland has long been enslaved by the priest and the king that Stephen Dedalus was so desperate to destroy inside his head. The elation of my first viewing of *The Butcher Boy* was that one saw those despotisms evaporate on the screen. The comfort that Sinead O'Connor brings to Francie at the end of the film is that Joe still loves him, that they are indeed blood brothers to the end of time.

It might be objected that fraternity is too masculine a word, but the real problem is that it is effectively archaic. The only current use of the word is in American English, where fraternity refers to exclusive societies of class privilege, a meaning which is the exact opposite of 1789's fraternity of all humanity. The best modern equivalent would be sisterhood and then the question that would need to be posed is whether we need two words or one. Siblinghood does not exist as a word and sibling itself is a technical term from anthropology and medical science with none of the emotional force of brother or sister.[36] It is worth noting, in this context, that *The Butcher Boy* is dedicated to McCabe's brothers and sisters; an acknowledgement of the bond for which there is no single name.

Paul Gilroy's planetary 'humanism'[37] is a term which attempts to reformulate, in a twenty-first century context, what fraternity invoked at the end of the eighteenth, but it might be objected that

Plate 8. Blood brothers till the end of time

the term is too bland and too abstract to capture a relationship modelled on the ties of blood. The film of *The Butcher Boy* developed, particularly in the maternal figure of Sinead O'Connor's Virgin Mary, an optimistic vision of the possibilities of Irish motherhood. It is not surprising that Jordan and McCabe's second collaboration, *Breakfast on Pluto* (2005), released as this book was being finished, concludes with both an abundance of new Irish mothers and a conversation between brothers, one of whom is a girl. To analyse that film fully, and particularly the process of adaptation, would take another book at least as long as this one. It is, however, worth noting that the relationship formed in the making of *The Butcher Boy* was so strong that Jordan was able to suggest to McCabe (and McCabe able to accept) that the story of Patrick 'Pussy' Braden recounted in the novel was not really finished. Furthermore, the pair of them then sat down to produce a screenplay which furnished both Pussy's reconciliation with the priest who had fathered him (a brilliant performance from Liam Neeson) and the discovery of his

75

mother Eileen in London. If one wanted one simple index of Jordan's uncanny ability to consider a mainstream audience without sacrificing the force of his original material, one could take the simple name change that Patrick Braden undergoes, the 'Pussy' of the novel becomes the 'Kitten' of the film.

It will be a question for future scholars and critics whether *The Butcher Boy* and *Breakfast on Pluto* are better considered as one work or as two. This book is devoted to *The Butcher Boy* and the process by which that book was adapted to the screen. In his great articles on adaptation, Bazin talked of how, in the best of cases, film adaptation and adapted book come to form a complicated whole. This, of course, is light years away from Shakespeare's adaptations, where the finished work has no active relation to the source text, but it constitutes one of the most striking features of our modern culture, from *A Streetcar Named Desire* to *Lord of the Rings;* from *The Grapes of Wrath* to *Fight Club;* from *Orlando* to *Blade Runner.* I would claim that *The Butcher Boy* is the most perfect example of this modern kind of adaptation.

CREDITS

Title:	*The Butcher Boy*
Director:	Neil Jordan
Release Year:	1997
Country	Ireland/USA

Cast:

Eamonn Owens	Francie Brady
Sean McGinley	Sergeant
Peter Gowen	Leddy
Alan Boyle	Joe Purcell
Andrew Fullerton	Philip Nugent
Fiona Shaw	Mrs Nugent
Aisling O'Sullivan	Ma Brady
Stephen Rea	Da Brady
John Kavanagh	Dr Boyd
Rosaleen Linehan	Mrs Canning
Anita Reeves	Mrs Coyle
Gina Moxley	Mary
Niall Buggy	Father Dom
Ian Hart	Uncle Alo
Anne O'Neill	Mrs McGlone
Joe Pilkington	Charlie McGlone
Pat McGrath	Farmer on Tractor
Jer O'Leary	Dublin Man
Pat Leavy	Dublin café Woman
Janet Moran	Dublin Shopkeeper
Paraic Breathnach	Man on Truck (as Páraic Breathnach)
John Olohan	Mr Nugent
Ardal O'Hanlon	Mr Purcell
Mikel Murfi	Buttsy
Brendan Conroy	Devlin
Tom Hickey	Gardener
Gregg Fitzgerald	Bogman #1
John Finnegan	Bogman # 2
Gavin Kelty	Bogman #3
Eoin Chaney	Bogman #4
Milo O'Shea	Father Sullivan

Sinead O'Connor	Our Lady/Colleen
Ciaran Owens	Boy at Fountain
Paolo Tullio	Mr Caffolla
Siobhan McElvaney	Girl in the Shooting Gallery
Aine McEneaney	Girl in the Shooting Gallery
Pat McCabe	Jimmy the Skite
Sean Hughes	Psychiatrist #1
Tony Rohr	Bogman in the Mental Hospital
Birdy Sweeney	Man in Well
Marie Mullen	Mrs Thompson
Stuart Graham	Priest at College
Macdara O'Fatharta	Alien Priest
Ronan Wilmot	Policeman
Vinne McCabe	Detective
Dermot Healy	Bogman in Hospital
Gerard McSorley	Psychiatrist #2
Neil Jordan	Executive Producer
Redmond Morris	Producer
Stephen Woolley	Producer
Neil Jordan	Screenplay
Patrick McCabe	Screenplay
Patrick McCabe	Original Novel
Elliott Goldenthal	Original Music
Adrian Biddle	Director of Photography
Mike Roberts	Camera Operator
Alan Butler	Focus Puller
Tony Lawson	Editor
Susie Figgis	Casting
Anthony Pratt	Production Design
Anna Rackard	Art Direction
Josie MacAvin	Set Decoration
Sandy Powell	Costume Design
Dee Corcoran	Hair Stylist
Eileen Buggy	Assistant hair stylist
Sandra Kelly	Assistant hair stylist
Morag Ross	Makeup Artist
Denise Watson	Makeup Trainee
Fiona Connon	Assistant makeup artist
Mary Alleguen	Production Manager
Breda Walsh	Production Coordinator

Des Martin	Unit Manager
Christopher Newman	First Assistant director
Suzanne Nicell	Second Assistant director
Barbara Mulcahy	Third Assistant director
Sarah Jordan	Trainee assistant director
Hugh Lane Spollen	Trainee assistant director
Suzanne McAuley	Trainee assistant director
David Balfour	Supervising Property master
Alex Bassett	Stand-by carpenter
Brian Bassett	Chief stagehand
Tommy Bassett	Construction manager
Mick Brownfield	Illustrator
Lisa Canty	Trainee art director
Triona Coen	Stand-by props
Colman Corish	Draughtsperson
Susie Cullen	Assistant art director
Gerry Drew	Master carpenter
Brendan Deasy	Sound recordist
Leonard Green	Assistant sound editor
Pauline Griffiths	Foley artist
Nina Hartstone	Assistant sound editor
Peter Holt	Foley editor
Kieran Horgan	Sound recordist
Andrea Isaac	Assistant sound editor
Eddy Joseph	Supervising sound editor
Jenny Lee Wright	Foley artist
Dominic Lester	Assistant sound re-recording mixer
Stephen McLaughlin	Music mixer
Stephen McLaughlin	Music recordist
Nigel Mills	Dialogue editor
James Nichols	Additional music recordist
Gerry Johnston	Special Effects technician
Charles J. Connon	Grip trainee
Neil Crawford	Stand-by rigger
Kevin Day	Gaffer
Gary Donague	Best Boy
Noel Donnellon	Video assist operator
Philip Fitzsimons	Rigging gaffer
David Grennan	Clapper Loader
Sorcha Hyland	Camera trainee
Pascal Jones	Chief rigger

Colin Manning	Camera grip
Bill Levins	Electrician
Albert Cassells	Electrician
Liam Moran	Electrician
Peter O'Toole	Electrician
Patrick Redmond	Still Photographer
Jens Baylis	Second assistant film editor
Peter Byrne	Assistant Location Manager
Lian Callaghan	Lead costumer
Maria Collins	Assistant production coordinator
Mary Crotty	Unit Publicist
Geraldine Daly	Location Manager
Jill Dempsey	Crowd casting
Diana Dill	Script Supervisor
Lisa Drayne	Production Trainee
Eamon Dunne	Action Vehicle Coordinator
Cara Gavigan	Assistant Location Manager
Grainne Gavigan	Lightwork assistant
Matthias Gohl	Music producer
Elliot Goldenthal	Orchestrator
Gerry Grennell	Dialogue Coach
Ken Hecht	Composer: song 'No One Knows'
Charmian Hoare	Dialogue coach
Maureen Hughes	Casting assistant
Gary Jones	Financial controller
John Kavanagh	Transportation coordinator
Louise Keating	Lead costumer
Bob Last	Music supervisor
Gaye Lynch	Second assistant film editor
Ernie Maresca	Composer: song 'No One Knows'
Richard Martinez	Electronic music producer
Ruth McMahon	Unit nurse
Eimer Ni Mhaoldomhnaigh	Assistant Costume Designer
Johnny Mulligan	Assistant accountant
Shane Munnelly	Transport department
Gary Nixon	Production accountant
Niamh O'Dea	Researcher
Emer Ó Laoghaire	Wardrobe trainee
Tricia Perrott	Assistant: Mr Morris
Brenda Rawn	Executive assistant: Mr Jordan
Nuala Roche	Assistant film editor

Mairead Sandford	production secretary
Yvonne Thunder	Assistant: Mr Jordan
Judith Williams	Wardrobe trainee
Philippa Wood	Assistant: Mr Woolley

Aspect Ratio:	1.85:1
Running Time:	109 mins
Colour Code	Colour

Endnotes

1. Edmund Spenser, *A View of the Present State of Ireland*, ed. W. L. Renwick (Oxford: Clarendon Press, 1970), p. 104.
2. It was a lecture given by Seamus Deane at Cambridge in early 1980 which first made me understand the importance of 'The Statues'.
3. It is this fact which makes the contemporary development of Irish Studies so interesting and which might be held to supply one of this new discipline's constitutive questions.
4. James Joyce quoted in Arthur Power, *Conversations with James Joyce*, ed. Clive Hart (New York: Barnes and Noble, 1974) p. 65.
5. See Declan Kiberd, *Inventing Ireland: The Literature of the Modern Nation* (London: Jonathan Cape, 1995), pp. 497–512.
6. For the distribution of pigs in relation to the size of farms, see Kevin O'Neill, *Family and Farm in Pre-Famine Ireland* (Madison: University of Wisconsin Press, 1984), p. 91.
7. There has been an enormous literature both personal and academic on abuse within the industrial schools; see Michael R. Molino, 'The "Houses of a Hundred Windows": Industrial Schools in Irish Writing', *New Hibernia Review*, Vol. 5, No. 1. (2001), pp. 33–52.
8. See Austin Woolrych, *Britain in Revolution* (Oxford: OUP, 2002), p. 675.
9. This historical moment is, of course, the setting for Brian Friel's great play, *Translations* (London: Faber & Faber, 1981).
10. There are some Irish speakers in Monaghan as late as the 1891 census but the county is predominantly English speaking by the end of the eighteenth century. See Brian O'Cuiv, *Irish Dialects and Irish-speaking Districts: Three Lectures* (Dublin: Institute for Advanced Studies, 1993), pp. 21–22.
11. From H. Montgomery Hyde, *Oscar Wilde* (London, 1976), quoted in Declan Kiberd, *Inventing Ireland* (London: Jonathan Cape, 1995), p. 35.
12. From Alessandro Francini Bruni, *Joyce intimo spogliato in piazza* (Trieste, 1922), quoted in Richard Ellmann, *James Joyce* (2nd edition) (Oxford: Oxford University Press, 1983) p. 217.
13. For the viciousness of the row see Michael Dwyer, 'Ten Days that Shook the Irish Film Industry', *In Dublin* (8 April 1982), pp. 19–24.
14. See Angus Finney, *The Egos Have Landed: The Rise and Fall of Palace Pictures* (London: William Heinemann, 1996).
15. For further details and references for this history, see Colin MacCabe, *Godard: A Portrait of the Artist at Seventy* (London: Bloomsbury, 2003),

pp. 66–76. On the concept of the author, see Colin MacCabe, 'The Revenge of the Author', in *The Eloquence of the Vulgar* (London: BFI, 1999), pp. 33–41.

16. André Bazin, 'Adaptation or the Cinema as Digest', in *Film Adaptation*, ed. James Naremore (New Brunswick: Rutgers University Press, 2000), pp. 19–27, and 'In Defense of Mixed Cinema', *What is Cinema*, Vol. 1, essays selected and translated by Hugh Gray (Los Angeles: University of California, 2005), pp. 53–75.

17. Angela Carter, *The Bloody Chamber* (London: Vintage, 1995), p. 118.

18. Paul Taylor and Steve Jenkins, 'Wolf at the Door', interview with Neil Jordan, *Monthly Film Bulletin*, Vol. 51, No. 608 (September 1984), p. 265.

19. Emer Rockett and Kevin Rockett, *Neil Jordan: Exploring Boundaries* (Dublin: Liffey Press, 2003), p. 104.

20. See Finney, *The Egos Have Landed*.

21. See Peter Biskind, *Down and Dirty Pictures: Miramax, Sundance and the Rise of Independent Film* (London: Bloomsbury, 2004), pp. 142–148.

22. In conversation with the author, November 1992.

23. See Colin MacCabe, 'Throne of Blood', *Sight and Sound*. Vol. 1, No. 6 (October 1991), pp. 12–14.

24. Jessica Scarlata 'Carnivals and Goldfish: History and Crisis in The Butcher Boy', in *Literature and Film: A Guide to the Theory and Practice of Film Adaptation*, ed. Robert Stam and Alessandra Raengo (Oxford: Blackwell, 2005), p. 235.

25. Jordan's sense of himself as an historian was clear when in January 1996 he savaged the leading revisionist historian Roy Foster on Irish radio for pontificating about *Michael Collins* when he had neither seen the film nor read the screenplay. Historians, insisted Jordan, were those who acquainted themselves with the primary sources before making judgements. See Neil Jordan's *Michael Collins Film Diary and Screenplay* (London: Vintage, 1996), p. 63.

26. 'Immature poets borrow; mature poets steal; bad poets deface what they take, and good poets make it into something better' (T. S. Eliot, *The Sacred Wood* (London: Methuen, 1960), p. 125).

27. For an overview of the debate about *Michael Collins*, see Keith Hopper, ' "Cat-calls from the Cheap Seats": The Third Meaning of *Michael Collins*', *Irish Review*, No. 21 (1997), pp. 1–28.

28. Luke Gibbons, 'Projecting the Nation', in *The Cambridge Companion to Modern Irish Culture*, ed. Joe Clery and Claire Connolly (Cambridge: CUP, 2005), p. 208.

29. Martin McLoone, *Irish Film: The Emergence of a Contemporary Cinema* (London: BFI, 2000), p. 217.

30. For the concept of rhyme in film see Stephen Heath, 'Film and System: Terms of Analysis', Part 1, *Screen*, Vol. 16, No. 1, pp. 7–77; Part 2, *Screen*, Vol. 16, No. 1, pp. 91–113.

31. The importance of this passage was pointed out to me by Keith Hopper. See his 'Patrick McCabe's *The Butcher Boy*', *OSCAIL Degree/Diploma in the Arts: Literature 6 Module* (Dublin: NDEC, 1996). pp. 1–18.

32. James Joyce, *Dubliners* (London: Penguin, 1956), p. 18.

33. For more details, see Marina Warner, *Alone of All Her Sex* (London: Vintage, 2000), p. 93.

34. For more details see Dana Och, 'The World Goes One Way and We Go Another: Movement, Migration and Myth in Irish Cinema', chapter 4 Pittsburgh PhD dissertation (2006).

35. The Irish Studies programme at Notre Dame has made Irish language compulsory for its doctoral students. While it is laudable to make such instruction available, one can imagine what Seamus Joyce would have said about the compulsion.

36. It is interesting that Anglo-Saxon is extremely rare among Indo-European languages in having a word, sibling, which covers brothers and sisters. Carl Darling Buck notes that 'special expressions for brother(s) and sister(s) are uncommon' (*A Dictionary of Selected Synonyms in the Principal Indo-European Languages* (Chicago: Chicago University Press, 1949), p. 108). The fact that 'siblinghood' does not occur in any Indo-European languages is one of the strongest linguistic arguments for a fundamental difference between the sexes.

37. See Paul Gilroy, *After Empire: Melancholia or Convivial Culture?* (London: Routledge, 2004).

Bibliography

Bazin, André. 'Adaptation or the Cinema as Digest', in *Film Adaptation*, ed. James Naremore. New Brunswick: Rutgers University Press, 2000. 19–27.

Behan, Brendan. *The Hostage*. London: Methuen, 1958.

Biskind, Peter. *Down and Dirty Pictures: Miramax, Sundance and the Rise of Independent Film*. London: Bloomsbury, 2004.

Buck, Carl Darling. *A Dictionary of Selected Synonyms in the Principal Indo-European Languages*. (Chicago: Chicago University Press 1949).

Carter, Angela. *The Bloody Chamber and Other Stories*. London: Vintage, 1995.

Dwyer, Michael. 'Ten Days that Shook the Irish Film Industry'. *In Dublin* (8 April 1982): 19–24.

Eliot, T. S. *The Sacred Wood: Essays on Poetry and Criticism*. London: Methuen, 1960.

Ellmann, Richard. *James Joyce*. 2nd edition. New York and Oxford: Oxford University Press, 1982.

Finney, Angus. *The Egos Have Landed: The Rise and Fall of Palace Pictures*. London: William Heinemann, 1996.

Gibbons, Luke. 'Projecting the Nation', in *The Cambridge Companion to Modern Irish Culture*. Eds. Joe Cleary and Claire Connolly. Cambridge: Cambridge University Press, 2005. 206–224.

Heath, Stephen. 'Film and System: Terms of Analysis, Part 1'. *Screen*, Vol. 16, No. 1 (1975): 7–77.

——. 'Film and System: Terms of Analysis, Part 2'. *Screen*, Vol. 16, No. 2 (1975): 91–113.

Hopper, Keith. ' "Cat-Calls from the Cheap Seats": The Third Meaning of Michael Collins'. *The Irish Review*, No. 21, Autumn/Winter (1997): 1–28.

——. 'Patrick McCabe's *The Butcher Boy*.' *OSCAIL Degree/Diploma in the Arts: Literature 6 Module*. Dublin: NDEC, 1996. 1–18.

Jordan, Neil. *Night in Tunisia*. 2nd edition. London: Chatto & Windus, 1983.

——. *The Past*. London: Jonathan Cape, 1980.

——. *The Dream of the Beast*. London: Chatto & Windus, 1983.

——. *Mona Lisa*. London: Faber & Faber, 1986.

——. *Angel*. 2nd edition. London: Faber & Faber, 1989.

——. *High Spirits*. 2nd edition. London: Faber & Faber, 1989.

——. *The Crying Game*. London: Vintage, 1993.

——. *Sunrise with Sea Monster.* London: Chatto & Windus, 1994.

——. *Michael Collins: Screenplay and Film Diary.* London: Vintage, 1996.

——. *Shade.* London: John Murray, 2004.

Joyce, James. *Dubliners.* London: Penguin, 1956.

Kiberd, Declan. *Inventing Ireland.* London: Jonathan Cape, 1995.

MacCabe, Colin. 'Throne of Blood', Sight and Sound Vol. 1 No. 6 (October 1991), pp. 12–14.

——. 'The Revenge of the Author', in *The Eloquence of the Vulgar: Language, Cinema and the Politics of Culture.* London: British Film Institute, 1999. 33–41.

——. *James Joyce and the Revolution of the Word.* 2nd edition. Basingstoke: Palgrave, 2002.

——. *Godard: A Portrait of the Artist at 70.* London: Bloomsbury, 2003.

Massey, Irving. *The Gaping Pig: Literature and Metamorphosis.* Berkeley: University of California Press, 1976.

McCabe, Patrick. *The Adventures of Shay Mouse: The Mouse from Longford.* Dublin: Raven Arts Press, 1985.

——. *Music on Clinton Street.* Dublin: Raven Arts Press, 1986.

——. *Carn.* Dublin: Aidan Ellis, 1989.

——. *The Butcher Boy.* London: Picador, 1992.

——. *The Dead School.* London: Picador, 1995.

——. *Breakfast on Pluto.* London: Picador, 1998.

——. *Mondo Desperado.* London: Picador, 1999.

——. *Emerald Germs of Ireland.* London: Picador, 2001.

——. *Call Me the Breeze.* London: Faber & Faber, 2003.

McLoone, Martin. *Irish Film: The Emergence of a Contemporary Cinema.* London: British Film Institute, 2000.

Och, Dana. 'The World Goes One Way and We Go Another: Movement, Migration and Myth in Irish Cinema' Pittsburgh PhD dissertation (2006).

O'Cuiv, Brian. *Irish Dialects and Irish-speaking Districts: Three Lectures* (Dublin: Institute for Advanced Studies), 1993.

O'Neill, Kevin. *Family and Farm in Pre-Famine Ireland: The Parish of Killashandra.* Madison: University of Wisconsin Press, 1984.

Power, Arthur. *Conversations with James Joyce.* Ed. Clive Hart. London: Millington, 1974.

Rockett, Emer and Kevin. *Neil Jordan: Exploring Boundaries.* Dublin: Liffey Press, 2003.

Scarlata, Jessica. 'Carnivals and Goldfish: History and Crisis in the Butcher Boy', in *Literature and Film: A Guide to the Theory and Practice of Film*

Adaptation, ed. Robert Stam and Alessandra Raengo. Malden, MA/Oxford: Blackwell, 2005. 235.

Sillar, Frederick Cameron, and Meyler, Ruth Mary. *The Symbolic Pig: An Anthology of Pigs in Literature and Art*. Edinburgh/London: Oliver and Boyd, 1961.

Spenser, Edmund. *A View of the Present State of Ireland*. Ed. W. L. Renwick. Oxford: Clarendon Press, 1970.

——. *The Faerie Queene*. Ed. A. C. Hamilton, text eds. Hiroshi Yamashita and Toshiyuki Suzuki. Harlow: Pearson Education, 2001.

Warner, Marina. *Alone of All Her Sex: The Myth and Cult of the Virgin Mary*. London: Vintage, 2000.

Woolrych, Austin. *Britain in Revolution, 1625–1660*. Oxford: Oxford University Press, 2002.